EXISTENTIAL TECHNICS

SUNY Series in Philosophy
Robert C. Neville, EDITOR

EXISTENTIAL TECHNICS

Don Ihde
*State University of New York
at Stony Brook*

State University of New York Press
ALBANY

FOR LINDA

Published by State University of New York Press, Albany

© 1983 State University of New York

All rights reserved

Printed in the United States of America

No part of this book may be used or reproduced in any manner whatsoever without written permission except in the case of brief quotations embodied in critical articles and reviews.

For information, address State University of New York Press, State University Plaza, Albany, N.Y., 12246

Library of Congress Cataloging in Publication Data

Ihde, Don, 1934-
Existential technics.

(SUNY series in philosophy)
Includes bibliographical references and index.
1. Technology—Philosophy. I. Titles. II. Series.
T14.I35   1983   601   82-10529
ISBN 0-87395-686-9
ISBN 0-87395-687-7 (pbk.)

10 9 8 7 6 5 4 3 2 1

Contents

Preface *vii*
Introduction *1*

Part One: TECHNICS

1. Technology and Human Self-Conception *9*
2. The Historical-Ontological Priority of Technology over Science *25*
3. The Technological Embodiment of Media *47*
4. Why Do Humans Think They Are Machines? *65*

Part Two: PERCEPTION

5. Phenomenological Variations and Artistic Discovery *81*
6. A Philosopher Listens *99*
7. Intercultural Perception *109*

Part Three: INTERPRETATION

8. Phenomenology and the Later Heidegger *119*
9. Interpreting Hermeneutics *137*
10. Phenomenology and Deconstructive Strategy *159*

Notes *183*
Index *189*

Preface

This book is a collection of essays grouped around three topics: Technics, or what might be called the human experience of technology; perception in both its sensory and cultural senses; and interpretation. I have gathered together these themes which are commonly discussed by those thinkers identified with phenomenology, hermeneutics, and, now, deconstruction. But I have tried to speak and write in such a way that the intelligent reader need not have an extensive technical background to gain from the issues.

As a collection one cannot expect either the systematic narrative found in books written as a totality, nor, perhaps the unity which goes with such books. Rather, what stands out is a series of contemporary questions grouped around the topics indicated. The essays included here span considerable time and geography in terms of their origins. "A Philosopher Listens," the oldest piece, goes back to 1971, and "Phenomenological Variations and Artistic Discovery" was originally presented to the British Society for Aesthetics. As indicated below, about half appeared or are scheduled to appear in diverse publications, but the other half have previously been given only in lecture form.

In spite of the discontinuity inherent in a collection, I hope that readers will note underlying and unifying concerns. Those concerns have long historical roots in the general philosophical inquiry into and reflection upon human experience and its constant transformations. From the heart of the phenomenological tradition, with which I am usually identified, comes the conviction that experience is focally that first-person experience which can be recalled and enticed reflectively. Moreover, with this tradition a sense of the primacy of the perceptual is retained. But perception is never bare perception and it collects itself interpretatively. These two themes are both ancient and found in all versions of philosophy. The third topic, *technics*, is a much more contemporary concern. By making our experience of technology thematic we increasingly find that our basic perceptions and interpretations are technologically textured, and that is the concern of the larger and dominant set of chapters here. *Existential Technics,* then, is a work in progress. It is an example of one philosopher's reflections upon contemporary life, hopefully connected to problems which are widely shared.

In terms of acknowledging help and criticism it is always difficult to know how to limit the circle of the most explicitly helpful persons. My colleagues in the department are always helpful and I should mention in particular Robert Neville, Patrick Heelan, David Dilworth, Donn Welton, and Drew Leder, each of whom read and responded concretely to parts or all of the essays. I am especially grateful to Linda Einhorn who helped edit my worst grammatical errors and infelicitous phrases. The circle is wider, and should include the departmental staff, other colleagues and students as well as the helpful critiques of the original audiences, but I hope that all will recognize my appreciation for such debts. Finally, I want to thank the State University of New York at Stony Brook for the release time which allowed me to complete much of the work included in this book.

Each of the following chapters was published in the books or journals indicated and is here reprinted with the publisher's permission.
1. "Technology and Human Self-Conception" was originally published in *The Southwestern Journal of Philosophy* 10, no. 1 (1979), 23–34.
2. "The Technological Embodiment of Media" appeared in *Communication Philosophy and the Technological Age,* edited by Michael J. Hyde and published by the University of Alabama Press (1982), pp. 54–72.

3. "A Philosopher Listens" appeared in *The Journal of Aesthetic Education* 5, no. 3 (1971), 69–76.
4. "Phenomenology and the Later Heidegger" appeared in *Philosophy Today* (Carthagena Station, Celina, Ohio 45822; Spring 1974), pp. 19–31.
5. "Interpreting Hermeneutics" was published in *Man and World* 13 (1980), 325–343.
6. "Phenomenology and Deconstructive Strategy" is scheduled to appear in the 1982 special issue of *Semiotica* on phenomenology and deconstruction.

Introduction

Technics is not a new word. Its best known use is probably to be found in the series of _____ and Technics books by Lewis Mumford. For a half a century Mumford has meditated upon the role of technology in human life from art to civilization. I like his choice of word because it conjures up a sense of *action* and *artifact* which I believe important for a focal understanding of technology. Technics stands in between the too abstract "technique" which can refer to any set action with or without a material object, and the sometimes too narrow sense of technology as a collection of tools or machinery.

Central to my understanding and use of technics is the sense of human action engaged with, through, among concrete artifacts or material entities. I wish to retain both a "hardware" reference for technology and yet not as some objectified realm apart from human action and interaction. In this collection I wish to underline even more clearly an aspect of the human response to our use of artifacts, hence *existential* technics. Existential technics, then, is the focus upon our experiential involvement with our own creation, technology.

Philosophers in North America have only begun to thematically focus upon the role technology plays in human life. In Europe there has been a longer tradition of philosophy of technology. Indeed, in the Marxist, phenomenological and existentialist traditions, technology has long been something of a preoccupation. In North America the preoccupation has been with science and we have long had a well-established philosophy of science tradition. The reasons for this contrast of emphases lie deeply embedded in the very traditions themselves. It is no accident that philosophy of technology has begun to emerge at just that time when the so-called Continental philosophies have come into their own in North America.

Continental philosophies are no longer "Continental" and there is a certain irony in this drift to North America. For what is common to the family of these philosophies is their focus upon and ultimate reference back to experience. Whether it is Marxism's concern with social experience (alienation), or existentialism's concern with the individual (anxiety), or phenomenology's with the structure of experience (intentionality), the root emphasis is there. The irony is that this emphasis was once a major American source in the only native philosophy, pragmatism. At least this was the case for Dewey, James and Mead.

This earlier concern, however, was eclipsed by the first turn to the Anglo-American philosophies of Positivism and later Analysis. The reduction of experience in Positivism and then the narrow focus upon linguistic phenomena served to place the native tradition in the background. Later, when the Continental philosophies arrived, the new form of reflection upon experience largely replaced what had been left of the native concern.

This collection of essays seeks to return to the philosophical reflection upon and critique of experience from a clearly American perspective, albeit out of the more precise analysis of experience made available through phenomenology. That is what unites the first set of essays on technics.

A brief picture of an academic office routine will indicate how intertwined our lives are with technics. Not only is there a plenum of machines (typewriters, telephones, dittos, xerox machines, air conditioners, lighting systems, etc., *ad infinitum*), but these are so familiar to us that we simply live among them in a taken-for-granted way. We direct many of our emotions to or through technologies (frustration over system breakdowns, fascination with new toys like word processors, anxiety over delays in communication, etc.) and yet rarely thematize technology as such as

Introduction

an existential element. Our daily lives are technologically textured for most waking moments.

What the first set of essays does, then, is to reflect upon some of those daily interactions and their effects upon us. But I do this with a certain emphasis. In an earlier collection, *Technics and Praxis* (Reidel, 1979), I was more concerned with outlining the types of interactions we have with artifacts or with what would be in phenomenological jargon, *noematic* description. In this collection I am more concerned with the reflexive turn to a *noetic* description. Given our engagement with the array of technologies, what does this do to the way in which we understand and interpret ourselves? If we take up our dwelling among machines, what does this do to our self-interpretation? The chapter titles are indicative of this concern.

The chapters addressed to technics are themselves diverse. Chapter One, "Technology and Human Self-Conception," is an attempt to show how self-interpretation is concretely situated. If Heidegger is right, as I believe he is, that humans are essentially self-interpreters, then historically we find ourselves in a new interpretative situation with respect to technology. This theme is taken up again in Chapter Four, "Why Do Humans Think They Are Machines?" In this case I am trying to show that philosophical critique makes interpretation a perpetual task as well as one which is filled with the dangers of too quick closure. Chapter Three, "The Technological Embodiment of Media," is an examination of that familiar set of technologies which structure a part of our life-world. Chapter Two with its somewhat ponderous title explores the philosophical thesis which underlies much of my thinking about technology and is a philosophical assertion of the primacy of action.

Part Two, "Perception," and Part Three, "Interpretation," might seem unrelated to the section on technics. And certainly in the essays contained in these parts technology plays no explicit role. But they are not unrelated. Much of my previous work has been concerned with perception and interpretation (hermeneutics) and takes its place in the phenomenological tradition of a concern for the life-world. Perception might well be called the concrete field where human action takes its shape. Certainly Edmund Husserl and Maurice Merleau-Ponty moved the philosophical notion of perception away from its passive empiricist sense into the realm of action and sensibility. I explore this activity in relation to artistic discovery in Chapter Five, there with a visual emphasis, and in a related way auditorily in Chapter Six. Chapter Seven continues the same interest at the intercultural level.

In terms of philosophical positions, if the assertion of the primacy of practice is what is dominant in the meditations on technics, then in the section on perception I am showing implicitly my conviction that it is variational method with respect to the topography of possibility which is the heart of a phenomenological investigation. Much in contemporary philosophy is trivial and too much is pedestrian—not that there shouldn't be some of this workmanship. But there is a question of balance and unlike the Wittgensteinian dictum that everything should remain the same after a philosophical analysis, I believe that philosophical activity should yield new perspectives. Variational method is precisely that activity, imaginative at its core, that systematically opens such perspectives. I give an example of that methodological activity in Chapter Five, "Phenomenological Variations and Artistic Discovery."

Part Three, "Interpretation," is more traditionally scholarly than investigative. In Chapter Eight I try to show that there is a deep unity to Martin Heidegger's thought and that precisely because he follows a phenomenological trajectory more radically than most philosophers, he finds it necessary to use language at its limits. Chapter Nine introduces and surveys some of the hermeneutic movement and situates it with respect to the contemporary philosophical world. Chapter Nine is my first attempt in writing to address the new deconstructionist movement, particularly in the thought of Jacques Derrida.

Deconstructionism appears to me as something of an enigma. Its own method owes a debt to ancestral phenomenology, and perhaps especially to a certain use of variational method. But it does so with motives which seem to me inimical to the very ex-

Introduction

periential reflectiveness which exemplifies the Socratic trajectory so central to phenomenology. What may be happening here is another ironic turn, this time in a drift towards the Continent by antiexperientialist strains of thought. Thus while Chapter Ten is the last in this collection, its word is but a first word.

Collections of essays have certain disadvantages. But they also have advantages among which is the sense of the more immediate work of the philosopher as he investigates, joins battles, reflects, addresses problems, theorizes and even plays. Thus while *Existential Technics* is diverse in the topics it includes, I am hopeful that it does display some of the enthusiasm, enjoyment and simultaneous seriousness which philosophy brings to those of us who become so engaged.

PART ONE
Technics

CHAPTER ONE
Technology and Human Self-Conception

I. Preface

Philosophy in its "platonist" and "idealist" form has tended to view technology pretty much as the outcome and result of ideas; or, to put it in contemporary form, technology is viewed as "applied science" with science in the form of theory as the root foundation of technology. This view, as I shall show in a moment, not only tempts the philosopher to overlook fundamental aspects of technology but leads to an arrival at questions of technology which is too late and thus misses the most fundamental questions.

There is, however, a set of traditions within philosophy that have already addressed technology at a fundamental level. Those philosophies are what I shall call the *praxis philosophies*. They include diverse families, such as Marxist and Critical Theory schools of thought, existentialism, phenomenology, and certain branches of American pragmatism. What they have in common are a starting point and conviction about human ontology. It is the conviction that some form of action precedes or grounds conception, or that a theory of action is primitive with respect to theory of knowledge.

Marx argues that human beings interact with their environment and with each other within some fundamental set of productive relations and actions—humans *are* what they make. For Sartre, humans project a project into the world and then seek to become that project—humans are what they do. For Dewey, humans are primarily problem-oriented, and their very intelligence is a tool for solving problems posed by their environment—humans are what they do in term of problems.

In each case some form of *praxis* is what grounds the relationship between humans and their world. Now when this thesis is applied to technology, not only can technology be seen to be important, and in a few cases even central, but it is related to the fundamental dimensions of human life itself. Thus philosophers in this tradition have argued that technology affects human nature, even if in some cases the effect is seen to be highly negative. Hans Jonas, for example, has specifically argued that technology affects the essence of humanity itself, and Heidegger as early as *Being and Time* argued for the primacy of the ready-to-hand as the origin and base for science itself. Such praxis philosophies are existential in that technology is implicated in the various dimensions of interactions between humans and their world. What I am after is an understanding of how humans *interpret* themselves within a technological culture, and the thesis which I shall argue is that technology supplies the dominant basis for an understanding both of the world and of ourselves. In setting up the case, I shall link a more general philosophical question: How do humans come to understand themselves? with a more specific thematic question: How does technology affect this process?

II. Method

Even before a philosophically informed analysis of technology and human self-conception, a minimal reflection can establish that technology at least provides a certain texture to the context of daily life. To make this point in class, I frequently assign students the task of cataloguing the number and kinds of human-technological artifact interactions in an hour or two of ordinary activity. The result is sometimes overwhelming and is a bit like trying to account for time in Proustian fashion. For example, beginning with the first conscious event of the day, it is likely that the ringing of an alarm or the sound of a clock radio is our first awareness. This is followed by a whole series of interactions and uses, which may include turning off the electric blanket or turning up the heat and in either case throwing back the technologically produced bedclothes from the technologically produced bed, engaging the vast plumbing system, and entering a veritable technological jungle in the modern kitchen with stove, toaster, hot-water system, lighting, and so on. And even the philosopher takes this technological texture for granted in his or her daily use of telephone, Xerox machine, typewriter, automobile, *ad infinitum*.

All of this is familiar, even if we do not critically reflect upon its meaning for human life. And if Heidegger is right, precisely because it is familiar it is even more difficult to elicit its existential significance. Such a technological texture to life forms a "life-world," and familiarity itself may be a clue or index for what is taken as "true." If humans always interpret the world and themselves in some dominant way, how do they do this in the midst of technology?

The framework into which I shall cast my inquiry is one derived from the insights of twentieth-century phenomenology, although I shall eschew any intensive or extensive use of its complex tribal language. But there are a few essential fundamentals of the model of interpretation which need be noted. I shall do this by contrasting a phenomenological framework for self-conception with what I take to be the more usually taken-for-granted framework that derives from Descartes.

Descartes's *cogito* stands historically for a method of interpreting the world and the self which derives from the formula *Cogito ergo sum*, "I think, therefore I am." His ideal of clear and distinct ideas grounded upon certainty may in one sense be said to have invented both the "subject" and the "external world." This is to say that when the *cogito*, "I think," became the basis for certainty it did so at a certain cost. On one side that cost was the world and existence became "external," and on the other the subject became self-enclosed. From the "I think," world had to be derived by means of the geometrical method of inference. The self, in turn, while apodictic, became privatized and closed off from the world.

Now this model of interpretation also contains a notion of what must be the case for self-conceptions or self-interpretation. The Cartesian *cogito* with its own self-evidence *knows itself immediately*; it is self-transparent in some sense. But this immediacy contrasts with whatever is now "out there" and which must now be constructed. I may model this notion of self-understanding in the following way:

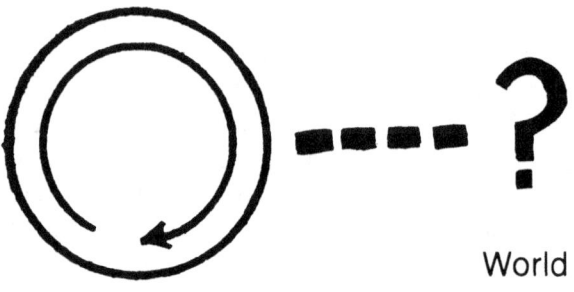

World

Self

Here the self knows itself directly by being self-contained and presumably transparent. But the world becomes doubtful, unknown, and external, and the relation between the "subject" and the "object" becomes an enigma. Historically, of course, the solution to the enigma was the introduction of the "geometric method," which infers the world.

Phenomenology, at its inception through Edmund Husserl, explicitly rejects the Cartesian understanding of both self and world and formulates a radically alternative model of the relation between self and world. In his *Cartesian Meditations*, Husserl seemingly enacts a quasi-Cartesian reduction through a method of "doubt" now called a suspension—but the result is one which is directly counter to the Cartesian result. Without examining the steps along the way, I shall turn to that contrasting result: First, Husserl finds that the subject always already finds itself in a world. And although that world is always "there" in some sense, it no longer is "external" in the Cartesian sense. It is *present*, and its presence is what is to be interrogated first. Second, the subject now turns out never to be empty or self-contained but already correlated with a world. Indeed, what is primitive is that correlation itself, a correlation which in later phenomenology takes the form of being-in-a-world. Third, the task of phenomenology, then, becomes the examination of the correlation which Husserl termed *intentionality*. Thus the model for interpretation which contrasts with the Cartesian model may be diagramed as:

Here what appears or presents itself first is world and that to which it presents itself is "self." But the mode and form of presentation are the relation itself, which is intentionality. Now what this means is that for every *cogito*, or act of thought, there is a reference, a something thought, which is a something. To say that there are no empty thoughts ultimately means that there is no worldless subject. Phenomenologically world and self are *equally* certain. But in terms of analysis there is a certain primacy to the world. Phenomenologically it is *from* the world that I come to understand myself. Thus it is in interaction with the world that I come to any form of self-understanding, contrarily, without world I would understand nothing. In contrast to Cartesian "subjectivism" phenomenology emerges as a new kind of relational "objectivism."

For our purposes, however, what is needed is a notion of how this correlation functions with respect to a coming to self-conception. This may be formulated simply as: if I am always already *in* a world, and if it is by means of the world that I came to understand myself, then there is an essential sense in which self-understanding is always tied to an understanding of a world. Here a modification must be introduced to the first diagram of the intentional correlation:

The intentional arrow turns out to be not single but interactional in form. It is both *projective*, a focused reference to world, and *reflective*, a movement from the world.

For interpreting self-understanding, the phenomenological self is seen to be neither self-contained nor separated from a context, a field, a world. In fact, to know oneself becomes a task, not a Cartesian given, since self-knowledge is no longer direct, autonomous, or self-contained.

My interpretation will follow this model of self-understanding, and I will examine certain specific features of what may be called a "technological world" and of self-understanding in that context. It will be suspected from the outset that, if self-knowledge is correlational or intentional, that something must happen at both ends of the relation with respect to human self-conception.

III. Technology and Human Self-Conception

If the intentional model of interpretation is the structure of phenomenology, the use of variations to isolate invariants is the dynamics of phenomenology. I shall use a set of variations in Husserlian style to point up what I believe are invariant features of human self-interpretation. The variants I shall use, however, are not strictly either the perceptual or the imaginative ones used in early phenomenological history. Rather I shall draw from both anthropological and history-of-religion disciplines to outline what may be called "world interpretations." I am seeking here an understanding both of what is variant and of what is invariant with respect to the ways human beings *project* and *reflect* a basic set of relations to a world.

What is not Husserlian in this analysis is that I am taking what I shall call *existential praxis* as a fundamental mode of human-world correlation. By this I mean a very broad, but concrete pattern of *actions* which always include relations with things of a material sort. Thus from the start I potentially include what come to be "technologies." The thesis is meant to illustrate both variations and invariants which relate to such human activities in the world.

To simplify the situation, I shall take only three somewhat idealized examples of a cultural human-world correlation with the specific "worlds" understood to be in scare quotes and seek to isolate what are the specific modes of understanding world and self in each example. My interpretation follows the phenomenological model of interpretation formerly outlined:

Variation 1

Imagine a somewhat idealized partly nomadic Amerindian society. It is a hunting and gathering society whose form of existential praxis is one which gains its living from hunting animals and gathering plants and their products, but it is not primarily a sedentary society which practices agriculture or animal domestication. First, what is the "world" which is projected? Obviously it is a "world" which focuses upon animal and plant life. Of it there must be genuine knowledge, and this takes the shape of knowing what is good to eat, what is useful as a product for shelter, clothing, and so on. In short, this society adapts in a particular, focused or—phenomenologically—intentionally shaped way. Its project includes knowing migratory routes, animal behavior, plant distribution, and other patterns. Its "world," in short, is that lively world of animals and plants to which human beings focally relate for existence itself.

I have already suggested that the focal understanding of this "world" will take a particular shape. At its center will stand those items of the world which are of particular concern to the inhabitants. But if we now turn to the reflexive side of this project, we may note how this pattern of concern takes the specific form of human self-conception that it does. Here we may undertake a play upon the notion of reflection. A "reflective activity" in such a society takes the form of ritual and ritually transmitted knowledge. And here examination of societies of this sort reveal an interesting phenomenon. Often the reflection specifically projects an idealized form of existential praxis into some nonordinary time or place in the form of cultic behavior. In this case we find specific cults—of the dog, the buffalo, the snake, and so on. Young males, potential hunters, are initiated by secret ritual and dramatized form into such cults, and from this they learn the patterns of existential praxis which in fact form the basis of the society's life. But in the esoteric ritual one factor stands out—the initiate identifies or becomes "like" that to which he is primarily related. Thus in such a society the Indian thinks himself to be "brother" to the cult animal or, generalized, to be "brother" to the animal kingdom.

Similarly, the young women of the tribe undergo counterpart ritual initiations in which plant life and its patterns often are internalized and related to the existential praxis of gathering, making, and so on. In short, the actual form of life which projects a certain relation to world in the form of a "world" of the Amerindian also reflects into an idealized mode this form, and from it emerges a type of self-understanding in which the human becomes "like" the "world" which is projected.

Variation 2

Now take an idealized agricultural society to note the form of life it takes. Here the existential praxis is changed. Both animal and plant life have been domesticated, and the basic patterns of life are those which revolve around a set of rhythms and relations which follow the cycles of grain and animal production. Now the familiar "world correlate" takes on an increasingly definite pattern in which constant repetition becomes basic and to which change is seen as a kind of threat.

The agricultural cycle is one of planting, growth, maturation, harvest, dormancy, and again planting. On the animal side there is a similar rhythm, more specifically related to sexual fertility in which there is birth, maturity, rutting and reproduction, slaughter, and again birth. This is the appearance of the ancient agricultural "world." The existential praxis is focused, and human beings here undertake and enhance those patterns which support life. But they also increasingly project this form upon a wider and wider set of phenomena—including, as we know, the projection of repeated cycles into the very heavens themselves as ancient agricultural society becomes urbanized and invents forms of astronomy and so on.

The ritual reflection of this form of life again takes the shape of humanity needing both to repeat its basic pattern of life and to be "like" that very "world" which is projected. The rites of agricultural society in ancient form are great cycle rites emphasizing fertility and identification with animal and plant life. The dying and rising gods, peasants copulating in fields to assure fertility, blood rituals of animal slaughter repeat and reinforce the very form of life which mirrors existential praxis.

At this point, however, both the variant and the invariant features begin to come clear, and variation 3 may be anticipated. Here it may be the case that objections begin to take shape precisely because we are quick to see where this leads. Both the Amerindian and the ancient agricultural variants, we might hold, are "primitive" and "prescientific" in that the apparent "anthropomorphization" of their "worlds" is too obvious to us. We have, we might hold, at least deanthropomorphized the world and thus are presumably nearer the truth than such "primitives." But if my thesis holds, we must apply the intention method equally to all variations to see what presents itself.

Variation 3

In this case the "world" is a technological one. What life-shape does it take, and how does "world" present itself and get understood? Of our dominant interpretation there can be little doubt. The contemporary "world" has been deanimated of both the nomadic and the agricultural projections. But, positively put, it has been mechanated. The "world" for us is interpreted as one of a vast system of impersonal relations, often explicitly conceived of in terms of mechanical metaphors. From Descartes on, the "world" has frequently been characterized as a "mechanism" which at one time was sometimes tinkered with by the Maker—but which today runs without tinkering. Even our bodies and those of animals were, and continue to be, interpreted along *technological* lines. We are contrivances of pumps (hearts), levers (arms), and electrical systems (nerves). What is this but a technological projection of "world"?

Furthermore, just as the Amerindian and the ancient agriculturalist became "like" their worlds through the projective-reflective process, we also internalize the external understanding. To understand itself is often to understand a "mechanism"; to follow rhythms of day and night must presuppose some form of "biological clock." Now although I could extend this virtually *ad infinitum*, the direction is clear enough. Do not our "world" and self-understanding in fact reflect the very form of existential praxis in which we have been engaged for several centuries?

To this point I have admittedly very sketchily made some suggestions, but a few preliminary observations may follow from these: First, I am suggesting that, far from clearly showing that twentieth-century life is superior to other forms of human life regarding self-understanding, I have suggested that the form of self-interpretation itself is *invariant* through all three examples. We project in terms of some focused form of existential praxis which influences, if not sets, the selected forms of knowledge which we will regard as central. Second, far from having de-anthropomorphized our "world" compared with those of the other two variations, we have created only a new form of "anthropomorphization" now in the form of a technologically projected "world." Third, the emergent form of self-understanding is one which functionally is exactly equivalent to the other two variations as a kind of reflection and internalization of the very projected "world" we find ourselves in.

This, however, is still suggestive. What I must now do is turn more specifically to the theme of technology and self-understanding and demonstrate more intensely that our form of *existential praxis* is itself basic for our "world" and show how this reflects itself in contemporary "ritual" life.

IV. A Technological "World"

Each of the variants sketched, I hold, contains genuine forms of knowledge. Amerindian nomadic societies knew the patterns of animal migration and behavior, often more thoroughly than even our contemporary territorialists do; ancient agricultural society not only came to know the cyclical patterns of plant and animal life but also invented a type of experimental genetics and breeding insights, just as we genuinely have come to know the vastly extended "mechanical" knowledge of the universe itself. Each projection aimed at the world carries with it a form of knowledge. And each projection reflects this back into the deeper form of life which revolves around the concrete praxis of the human "lifeworld." But the problem for the inhabitant of any given "world" is that it is so familiar to him or her that little distance is to be found. The familiar is simply taken as the "true."

To gain distance and insight one needs to see the variants within one's own "world" against a deeper, invariant structure, a structure which both takes account of the objective societal relations and can point up the forms of imaginative projection which depict the ideals and aims of the human world.

It is clearly not the case that we are lacking these insights altogether. For example, the social sciences have developed certain means of analysis which have pointed up some of the factors I have already alluded to. Focally, the ancient agricultural variant of a human world may be seen to be dependent upon the reiteration and repetition of a certain cyclical pattern which is repeated from the farmer, who repeats and practices the cycle of agriculture, all the way to the specific *interest* groups which symbolize the form of life, as for example a priesthood or royalty who ritually enact the fertility and renewal rites of the society.

Here the question naturally arises, how does this projection, repetition, and ritual renewal take place in our form of technological life? The recent lengthy discussions of alienation, depersonalization and anomie as resulting from or at least associated with technological society point to a certain lack of adjustment suffered by contemporary human beings in this "world." But

TECHNICS

where do we affirm and reenact our current existential praxis? What are our rituals of identification with the "world" we are projecting? Clearly we have nothing like either the esoteric initiation rituals or the annual repetition of the New Year's festivals which repeat the sacred time of agricultural society.

What is needed here, however, is to understand the functional nature of ritual as an imaginative projection-reflection. What happens functionally in affirming a self-understanding is that some form of existential praxis is projected into a not-now or other or sacred time and place and is then reflected back upon the inhabitants of a "world." And while it is the case that the first variant projected such an imaginative action into an esoteric realm and the agricultural society projected the same into an ancient pretime, as might be expected with technological time, we project our self-understanding into an *irreal future* time.

Permit me here a final and only partly cryptic speculation to illustrate what I take to be a certain fascination with technological self-understanding. Our "ritual," like all past ritual, is most appropriate if it is conveyed dramatically in clothing appropriate for our form of life. Just as the snake dancer or the eagle dancer creates the impression of a sacred and dramatized being, or as the cyclical birth-and-death rituals encapsule existential praxis in the New Year's festival, each embodying the imagination in a form appropriate to the respective "world" reflected, so we might expect our "ritual" to be embodied.

I therefore suggest that ours is embodied in various technological representations, the most notable candidates being film and television. And here I engage a bit of fancy to make a point: the current fascination of utopias, science fiction, UFOs, and such phenomena as *Star Wars*, *Battleship Galactica*, and the like illustrates a genre of projections placed in irreal future time. I propose that we take these momentarily as examples of rituals of self-interpretation and see what they say.

If they are instances of "ritual," they can at least be interpreted to show certain patterned notions which do relate to contemporary self-conceptions. I shall take account of only a few of these. First, note the role of what may be called "nature" compared with "culture" in the genre. Nature is at best a background, often spectacular but not itself a force to be reckoned with. Its limits have been conquered, including the absolute limit of our present science, the speed of light. What is foreground is totalized culture. Life takes shape within and often literally inside various forms of technological cocoons. Home is a spaceship. Outside one must wear a miniaturized spaceship in the form of a space suit. These rituals project a totalized technology which becomes the marvelous but then familiar home for future human beings. Never mind that future technology does not seem plagued with the constant repair, entropy, and breakdown of ours.

This idealized projection, however, is also a reflection of *present* existential praxis. The spaceship as "home" is a projection of the present ideal of the totally self-contained and hence totally controlled environment. This direction can be instanced in architecture. At Stony Brook the new Health Sciences Center, which looks like something out of an Antonioni movie, is a monstrous set of building many stories high—but it has virtually no windows. In the "megastructure" which is the main building, the windows it does have actually open either to hallways or to the floor where the heating and cooling machinery is installed (only elite physicians' offices have corner oval windows). The rationale, of course, is total control over the environment, and thus the self-enclosure. The hospital on the other hand does have windows. I asked someone why that was the case—were they being humane to patients? The answer was, "No, we would have preferred a windowless hospital, too, but state law requires windows in hospitals." My point is that the projection of the ideal future world, the spaceship inside of which humans live, move, and have their being, is an expression of current existential praxis. Moreover, this self-contained technological environment is not only instanced in buildings but approximated in such items as the mini-environments of such things as contemporary recreational vehicles, which take technological suburbia, complete with TV, flush toilets, gas cookers, and the rest right into the wilderness. Such technological cocoons exemplify the trajectory of our civilization to totality.

If "home" is the technological cocoon, what becomes of the

"outside" which was nature? In the genre of projections mentioned, it is background, but in function it is something else. It is the realm of *resources*, not just there presumably for human use but there as stored energy. And nature, too, is to be reordered and transformed. Modernization includes the recording of everything from a transportation system to fully developed agriculture with transformed seeds (hybridization) planting processes (fertilizers and pesticides) to products (white bread). Ultimately nature in its untransformed state is inverted and taken into the totality of technological culture in the form of natural museums. Wilderness areas are functionally large pictures in the museums, set aside for temporary enjoyment and relaxation or escape from daily life, but episodic with respect to the cultural and "normal" world of technologically transformed nature. Thus the ultimate victory of technological totalization would be this inversion in which nature is itself taken into culture. Then technological civilization would be complete, and we would be "one" with our "world."

V. Summary

The somewhat, but only somewhat, facetious examples I have been tracing are not meant to complete a picture of what human self-understanding would be in technological civilization, nor are they really meant to cast a negative tone on our form of life. They are instead intended to illustrate the one and only thesis I have been developing: that all self-interpretation takes its shape in a certain way with respect to some basic form of existential praxis which is projected upon the world and reflected back in ways which become dominant ways of understanding ourselves and our world.

I have tried to show that, far from being obviously and self-evidently superior in attaining self-knowledge—a worthy Socratic goal—we remain caught in some degree in precisely the dyanamism which characterized the seeming "anthropomorphizations" of the other variants. We end up modeling ourselves upon the very "world" we project and interpret ourselves in terms of technology.

Negatively, there is also a point not developed here. If human beings are, as the existentialists have claimed, always transcendent beings, then what is needed more than ever is a way of attaining a transcendence to any reduction which ties us too closely to a "world" in which we continually fall into some interpretation which forecloses us in a totality. What is needed is what I shall call a "loose" or maybe even "Zen" relation to technology.

CHAPTER TWO
The Historical-Ontological Priority of Technology over Science

I. Introduction

The thesis I wish to explore in this essay is that *there is a significant sense in which technology may be seen to be both ontologically and historically prior to science*. There is, of course, an obvious and trivial sense in which this claim may be regarded as true. If technologies in the broadest and most concrete sense involve humans and their uses of tools and artifacts, then at the least one can say that technology in this sense is both universal and probably used at the time of the arising of the human species. There are no instances of societies, cultures, or human groups which do not use tools and artifacts in their relations with the natural environment.

And if science centrally involves a theorizing about things in a systematic and hypothetical sense, then it should be apparent that the practiced and skilled uses of technologies long precede the kind of self-awareness implied in science. In the most general sense then, *praxis* precedes explicit theory.

I wish, however, to suggest that there is a more specific sense in which technology, particularly in its more recent developments, is the *condition of the possibility of science*. I argued in *Technics and Praxis* (Reidel, 1979) that science, in its contemporary sense as an experimental science wedded to specific meanings of measurement, is *necessarily embodied* in its instrumentation. Indeed, one of the chief differences between modern science and Greek contemplative science lies in the development of instrumentation both for measurement and for actual investigative purposes. I showed how instrumentation extends and embodies perception.

Historically, of course, even Greek science in actual practice engaged some measurement technologies. But the lack of a specific technological impetus also doomed Greek science to its primarily speculative attainments (witness the odd ideas about the shapes of atoms and causes of sweet, bitter, or sour tastes in Democritus. Lacking any means of investigation of such micro-phenomena, the speculation had to remain just that). This lack of appropriate technology determined the limits of a primarily contemplative science.

Here I wish to push the essential interlocking of science and technology further by arguing for the historical-ontological priority of technology as a condition of the possibility of science. I shall develop three unequal stages in this demonstration: First, I shall briefly describe what I take to be the standard and dominant theory of the relationship between technology and science. Second, I shall pay my debts to two important intellectual predecessors of my views. The philosophical debt is owed to Martin Heidegger, who may be said to have originated and solidified what has become the philosophy of technology for the twentieth century, and who argued most explicitly for the ontological priority of technology over science. The historical debt is owed to the large body of work done by Lynn White, Jr., who made us aware that there was a virtual technological revolution in the Middle Ages which preceded and laid the groundwork for the rise of modern science in the Renaissance and through the Enlightenment. The third step will then be an examination of certain aspects of the historical technological life-world. I shall develop this account along phenomenological lines.

II. The Standard Theory

There are a variety of conceptual possibilities which could account for the relationship of technology and science, but two extreme cases—I shall call them the "idealist" and "materialist"

The Historical-Ontological Priority of Technology over Science

interpretations—have the advantage of posing the issues most starkly.

What I shall call the idealist view is the interpretation which holds that science precedes and founds technology. It is an interpretation which holds that requisite for creating a (modern) technology, one must have insight into the laws of nature, a conceptual system at the formal and abstract level, and the ability to *apply* this knowledge to the material realm, thus creating a technology.

In this interpretation, technology follows from science, both ontologically as an application of scientific knowledge and historically as the spread of this insight into ever-widening realms of material construction.

The standard view is accompanied by an interpretation of the history of modern science and technology which may be characterized as follows: After a long dark period in European history, a revival of the Greek scientific spirit emerges within and animates what we call the Renaissance. Europeans regain an interest in nature, speculate about nature and evolve a method of understanding nature which we call Modern Science. Historically this movement becomes dramatic and fulfilled in such figures as Galileo, Kepler, Copernicus and eventually becomes fully systematized with Newton.

The rise of Modern Science is a development which includes (a) the discoveries of more sophisticated mathematics; (b) a gradual move away from religious and theological notions and a move towards a more mechanistic and materialist metaphysics; (c) a method which diverges from the more speculative ancient roots towards a more experimental and verification direction; and (d) a movement which results in the rise of physics as the primary science or at least the science which is first among equals.

Only after this historical development of science does there arise a technology (in the modern sense). The Industrial Revolution of the past century and a half and the explosion of the current "high technology" are plausibly dependent upon the precondition of scientific theory. Technology in the contemporary sense seems to spin forth almost directly from science itself.

In this essay I am not interested in a further exposition of the implicit metaphysics of this interpretation, nor am I going to undertake a direct attack upon its presuppositions. As an interpretation of the relationship between science and technology it has both plausible and implausible aspects. I shall point out some of these, but I shall do so indirectly by elaborating a strategy which this view must entail.

What must technology be, how must it appear if this view is correct? First, what will pass for technology must in the paradigm case be a technology which is obviously dependent for its shape upon scientific-theoretical considerations. Thus, the best examples are what we call today high technologies. While I do not intend what follows to be exhaustive by way of definition, I suspect a high technology must be characterized as a technology which must include: (a) a complex and interlocked system; (b) workings which are understood only by way of scientifically derived theories; (c) components which contain esoteric compounds and units, themselves the result of complex and scientifically determined processes; and (d) microscopic machine tolerances, internal organization, mechanical or electronic motions developed from micro-levels of manufacture and planned construction. A computer is an obvious case of such a high technology, but there are dozens of other examples which could do as well.

In contrast, "low" or, better, traditional technologies would be those which are simple, arrived at through a process of trial and error, which contain only rough interrelations of parts, and are understandable by any mechanically inclined person. A waterwheel is an example of such a technology.

That there is an apparent and even dramatic difference between the computer and the waterwheel seems clear. But just what and how that difference is to be accounted for is precisely what needs note. However, at the level at which I am developing the case, we need to be aware that the idealist position which holds that science is the condition of technology must accentuate a sharp difference between a presumed prescientific and scientific technology. In short, contemporary technology is seen to be disjunctive with traditional technology.

This tactic is conceptually necessary because otherwise one would have no way of accounting for the previously noted historical situation in which all peoples and societies use and have technologies whether or not they have a science in our sense. The historical dependence of technology upon science then becomes a special case of dependence; only *scientific* technology is historically dependent upon science.

The relationship of the Renaissance and Enlightenment periods to the Medieval Period may be seen to be an instance of the focus upon the assumed priority of science in the modern sense. Put most simply, because scientific knowledge as theoretical knowledge was assumed to be higher than so-called practical knowledge, the possibly unique attainment of the Middle Ages was overlooked.

III. A Materialist Theory: Heidegger and White

A contrary position is possible. I shall construct such a view by combining the insights of Martin Heidegger and Lynn White, Jr.

Martin Heidegger is perhaps the philosopher who has most originally and profoundly rendered the question of technology a central concern of philosophy. The position he developed in "The Question Concerning Technology" is one which argues for the ontological, but not the historical priority of technology over science. The argument is complex and I shall look at only a few elements of it.

Heidegger holds that Technology has always underlain what we have called science in the West, but it has been revealed as the origin of science only recently. Embedded in this complex argument, however, is a deep ambiguity about what shall count as technology. On the ontological level, Technology—more precisely the essence of technology—is a certain way of experiencing, relating to and organizing the way humans relate to the natural world.[1] On the historical level, at least in the chronological sense, Heidegger seems to grant that technology in its modern sense is "later than" science. In short, Heidegger accepts in some degree the notion that modern or scientific technology is essentially and distinctly different from traditional technology. I hold that he is wrong in allowing himself to accept this notion, and as a result he weakens his own case in such a way to give credence to the usual accusation that he is somewhat "romantic" with respect to technology. In sum, the Heideggerian position is that Technology, while ontologically prior to science, is historically later.

At the core of the view which Heidegger is espousing, lies an inversion of the standard view of the relationship between science and technology. This inversion is most dramatically illustrated by his claim that rather than technology being a tool of modern physics, it is exactly the opposite: physics is the necessary tool of Technology. In this first instance, Heidegger discerns that modern physics is necessarily interrelated with its instruments:

> It is said that modern technology is something incomparably different from all earlier technologies because it is based on modern physics as an exact science. Meanwhile we have come to understand more clearly that the reverse holds true as well: modern physics, as experimental, is dependent upon technical apparatus and upon progress in the building of apparatus. The establishing of this mutual relationship between technology and physics is correct. But it remains a merely historiographical establishing of facts and says nothing about that in which this mutual relationship is grounded.[2]

Then, in a much stronger statement, Heidegger argues that physics is the herald of Technology:

> Modern science's way of representing pursues and entraps nature as a calculable coherence of forces. Modern physics is not experimental physics because it applies apparatus to the questioning of nature. The reverse is true. Because physics, indeed already as pure theory, sets nature up to exhibit itself as a coherence of forces calculable in advance, it orders its experiments precisely for the purpose of asking whether and how nature reports itself when set up this way.[3]

The Historical-Ontological Priority of Technology over Science

This inversion, clearly evidenced in the way Heidegger views the relationship between science and technology, is one which nevertheless retains at least one partial sense in which science precedes technology. (I am quite aware, with most Heidegger scholars, of the distinction between *Historie* and *Geschichte* in Heidegger's use. However, *Geschichte* serves a specifically ontological function.)

This residual sense in which science historically precedes technology also accounts for a distinction between scientific and traditional technology. The strongest statement concerning this residual sense states:

> Chronologically speaking, modern physical science begins in the seventeenth century. In contrast, machine-power technology develops only in the second half of the eighteenth century. But modern technology, which for chronological reckoning is the later, is, from the point of view of the essence holding sway within it, historically earlier.[4]

Similarly, the disjunctive sense which the standard view must maintain and which separates modern from traditional technology, is allowed by Heidegger:

> The revealing that rules modern technology is a challenging, which puts to nature the unreasonable demand that it supply energy which can be extracted and stored as such. But does this not hold true for the old windmill as well? No. Its sails do indeed turn in the wind; they are left entirely to the wind's blowing. But the windmill does not unlock energy from the air currents in order to store it.[5]

And again, Heidegger, as he so frequently does, contrasts the peasant's sense of earth from that of the modern technologist's:

> In contrast, a tract of land is challenged in the hauling out of coal and ore. The earth now reveals itself as a coal mining district, the soil as a mineral deposit. The field that the peasant for-

merly cultivated and set in order appears different from how it did when to set in order still meant to take care of and maintain.[6]

Thus while we have the assertion of the ontological priority of Technology over science as an inversion of the standard view, a secondary sense is retained in which technology chronologically follows the development of science and a sense in which there is a disjunctive difference between traditional technology and modern technology. Science, in Heidegger's view, stands as the event which finally shows to us what Technology is ontologically. Science is the herald of Technology in a (chronological) historical sense:

> The modern physical theory of nature prepares the way not simply for technology, but for the essence of modern technology. For such a gathering-together, which challenges man to reveal by way of ordering already holds sway in physics. But in it that gathering does not yet come expressly to the fore. Modern physics is the herald of enframing, a herald whose origin is still unknown.[7]

What holds this argument together lies in the several ways in which Heidegger uses the term technology.

What may be called the suface definition of technology is what Heidegger calls the anthropological-instrumental understanding of technology, technology as a mere tool of science.[8] This definition, not false, is only merely correct. It does not reveal the *essence* of technology.

A second definition derives from the Greek *technē*, and begins to more nearly approximate the Heideggerian sense of Technology in that *technē* is both a name for the activities and skills of a craftsman and for the arts of both mind and hand, but also is linked to creative making, *poiēsis*.[9] For the Greeks *technē* was a production which was a kind of knowledge.

The third, and ultimate Heideggerian definition of Technology, however, makes of Technology a mode of truth or revealing (*alētheia*). Technology, in essence, reveals a world in a certain way. "Every bringing-forth is grounded in revealing."[10] "Technology is a mode of revealing, Technology comes to presence in the realm where revealing and unconcealment take place, where *alētheia*, truth, happens."[11] The essence of technology allows us to see, to order, to relate to the world in a particular way. Nature becomes standing-reserve, a source of energy for human use, and this mode of relating to the world becomes, in a technological era, the dominant and primary way in which we understand world.

I shall not further explore the Heideggerian view, except to note that only after Technology is discovered to be this way of relating to the world may one begin to understand how science, under this mode, is seen to be the necessary "tool" of Technology. Science becomes a means of knowledge which gives power, science becomes Baconian. And with this move the inversion is completed: Technology as the revelation of the world as standing-reserve is the ontological presupposition and ground of modern science.

Philosophically things would have been neater and clearer were it the case that Technology could be shown to be not only ontologically, but historically prior to science. And this would especially be so if the historical priority were of such a nature as to be understood as an experiential condition of the possibility of modern science. Such a view would also have the advantage that it would be continuous with the ordinary observation that some form of technology is universal and occurs wherever there are human societies.

I think this is the implicit import of the work of Lynn White, Jr., who has clearly caused a revision of the way in which we understand the Medieval period with respect to technology.

White's publications concerning Medieval technology span two decades. The landmark book, *Medieval Technology and Social Change* (1962), shows how technological development was deeply implicated in systems of warfare (the stirrup led to mounted shock warfare, thence to changes in social structure in Feudalism), agriculture (one plough combined with horse power and the development of three-field rotation led to a shift of food production to Northern Europe) and in that increasing hunger for mechanical power which laid the basis for other forms of increased productivity.

By looking at the burgeoning technology of the Medieval Period, White paints a historical picture of a Europe rapidly changing, avidly searching for inventions; and particularly hungry for power. This is the case with the newly invented mechanical devices for extracting power from water and wind. By 983 water power was being used for fulling mills, but within a century the *Domesday* census revealed that there were already 5,624 water mills in operation in England (a harbinger of the Industrial Revolution centuries later).[12] The windmill was referred to as early as 1180 and was common in much of Europe by 1240. The search for power in the Middle Ages utilized every source. Inventions from foreign lands were rapidly experimented with in new ways, often in practical, but rarely overlooked. This medieval search for power laid the groundwork for later industrial technology but it was also intricately tied to a search for knowledge. Giovanni da Fontana, for example, in 1420, designed the forerunners of our robot measurers in the form of swimming fish, flying birds, and running rabbits, all linked to a plan to measure surfaces and distances in water, the air and out-of-the-way places.[13]

One dramatic technological development during this period, a development which transformed the human perception of time, was the clock. In White's words, "Suddenly, towards the middle of the fourteenth century, . . . clocks seized the imagination of our ancestors . . . No European community felt able to hold up its head unless in its midst the planets wheeled in cycles and epicycles, while angels trumpeted, cocks crew, and apostles, kings, and prophets marched and countermarched at the booming of the hours."[14] Time and the movement of the spheres was tied to a mechanical device. And thus by 1382 the universe itself began to be conceived of according to a mechanical metaphor:

> It is the works of the great ecclesiastic and mathematician Nicholas Oresmus, who died in 1382 as Bishop of Lisieux, that we first find the metaphor of the universe as a vast mechanical clock created and set running by God so that "all the wheels move as harmoniously as possible." It was a notion with a future: eventually the metaphor became a metaphysics.[15]

White's more recent works have taken account of the unique intellectual climate which encouraged technological development in Europe. By the time of his publication, "Cultural Climates and Technological Advance in the Middle Ages," White can claim, "The technological creativity of medieval Europe is one of the resonant facts of history."[16] What he finds is that Medieval Europe was highly receptive to the use and development of technology and that several factors encouraged this: The organization and climate for order, stemming from the earlier Monastic reforms, readily adapted technology. The clock, used first to establish the order of time, agricultural techniques, and machines to lighten labor were all affirmatively valued. Indeed, his survey of the literature of the time finds that detractors from the praise of technology are rare. Contrarily, praise of invention, machines and their use is the rule.

Prior to our Bishop Oresmus who declares the heavens to be clockwork, one finds praise and prediction concerning a glorious technological future common: "Roger Bacon, 1260, pondering transportation, confidently prophesied an age of automobiles, submarines, and airplanes."[17]

This attitude of fascination and obsession with the technological stands in stark contrast to other areas of Christian civilization. Whereas the Latin West from the monasteries on accepted technology into the precincts of the holy—every cathedral must have a clock—the Eastern regions forbade such inventions in sacred space. Clocks must remain outside the realm of eternity, thus outside the church in the Orthodox lands.[18]

The positive evaluation of inventiveness, linked to a desire for machine power, was also accompanied by the willingness to adapt ideas and artifacts from any culture. What became the bow for our string instruments came from Southeast Asia. A Tibetan prayer-wheel may have inspired the windmill, and so the list goes. In short, the Medieval Period was suffused with interest in, desire for, and the development of technologies.

By the late Middle Ages, at the dawn of the time for the rise of modern science, White points out:

About 1450 European intellectuals began to become aware of technological progress not as a project (. . . this came in the late thirteenth century) but as an historic and happy fact, when Giovanno Tortelli, a humanist at the papal court, composed an essay listing, and rejoicing over, new inventions unknown to the ancients. . . . It was axiomatic that man was serving God by serving himself in the technological mastery of nature. Because medieval men believed this, they devoted themselves in great numbers and with enthusiasm to the process of invention.[19]

In short, White established that by 1500, a period whose image is consolidated by the technological genius of Da Vinci, there is a self-awareness of technology, the process of invention, and the desire to master Nature through human artifacts.

By the year 1500, Europe had already developed some of the instrumentation so fundamental to the very investigative possibility of science in the modern experimental sense. Lenses were invented by 1050, compound lenses by 1270, spectacles by 1285 and, by 1600, Gallileo's period, the microscope and telescope. Clocks, essential to measurement, began to be developed in the ninth and tenth centuries and by the 1500s were widespread from cathedral to town hall to individual watches.

On the industrial side one can note that Europe is by this time covered with wind and water mills; the lowlands were being drained by wind power; there were railways in mines; and the massive, sophisticated architecture of cathedrals, suspension bridges and other large projects were part of daily life. Yet, in spite of the now reflective obviousness of this pervasive technological achievement of the Middle Ages, White is probably right in still claiming that, "the scholarly discovery of the significance of technological advance in medieval life is so recent that it has not yet been assimilated to our normal image of the period."[20]

IV. The Historical-Ontological Priority of Technology

If one combines the claims of Heidegger concerning the ontological priority of technology with those of White concerning the immediately preceding historical technological revolution, one arrives at this essay's thesis. However, to consolidate this thesis I shall speculatively develop something of a phenomenology of daily life, first as it appeared in the European life-world, then as a variation, as it appeared in a different culture, that of the Polynesians. In so doing I shall focus upon spatial and temporal orientations.

A. A "Reconstruction" of an Aspect of the Medieval Lifeworld

My strategy in this reconstruction of a Medieval life-world will be to focus upon selected experiential components as they are embodied in praxis. It should be obvious by now that in the late Medieval Period mechanical contrivances were very common and indeed pervasive in many ordinary activities. The world was already implicitly thought of in terms of mechanical metaphors. But in my focus upon space and time I am concerned with the way these dimensions are *perceived*.

I begin with the familiar example of clocks, which were common in daily life in the late Medieval world. Lewis Mumford in his 1936 book, *Technics and Civilization* (New York: Harcourt, Brace and World), has already noted how the clock was crucial to the development and reorganization of Medieval life. According to Mumford, clocks were first commonly used in conjunction with monastic life and the development of disciplined and common order. The keeping of hours for religious exercises and the ordering of work set the pace for public or intersubjective life. Heidegger, too, in *Being and Time* (Harper and Row, 1962, German original in 1927) pointed out the way in which clocks are not mere artifacts, but "take account" of human surroundings and nature. One can say that once clocks are developed, we begin to perceive time through technology.

Take careful note of the specific perceptual representation of time via the clock. First, until recently, all clocks represent time through a use of moving pointers. This is the case whether one regards the moving shadow of the sundial, the linear scale of the early water clocks, or the eventual round cyclical face of the cathedral clock. I would point out here that this representation of time is one which has both a focus—the instant of time which is the precise "now" as that point where the pointer "stands"—and a duration or span of time within which the instant finds its place. The field or span of time is the spread of the clock face, whether linear or circular. Thus "now" takes its place within a duration of time.

If one begins to reflect upon the evolution of the clock, one can note the following distinct developments: at first the movement of the pointer is crude and relates primarily to fairly large "units" of time. The earliest circular faces of clocks were marked only into hours and had only one hand. But as clockwork became more mechanically refined, time was divided into smaller and smaller units; a second pointer was added to mark the minutes, and then a third to mark the seconds. Time was more and more quantified. This quantification was gradually more finely divided and the perception of time became even more open to finer discriminations, to what may be called the micro-features of time. Moreover, these micro-features could be considered atomistically as units which were discrete from each other. In short, the clock allows us to perceive time latently as a series of atomized, discrete instants, a representation of what was to become a "scientific" mode of analyzing time. Time is perceived via or through the clock and this perception is a technologically mediated perception.

Historically, what eventually became more and more important was the focal point of technologically mediated time. The instant of its micro-features stands out. It becomes the means for further investigating things and is now essential for contemporary scientific measurement. Simultaneously, but almost unnoticeably, the field of time, which is the background but grounding feature of clock time, recedes and becomes less important. This development reaches a qualitatively different result in the contemporary invention of the digital clock. The digital clock represents only the focal instant of time, the field of time is no longer perceptually represented and in the process the perception of time also changes. The person who awaits the train, who once could glance at his watch and *see* that it was yet ten minutes until arrival time by *seeing* the relation between the pointers and the span, now sees only the number and must infer or calculate the span. This is to say that the mental operation for telling the time changes, even if unnoticeably, with the digital clock. What this portends for us, I shall not now predict other than to observe that if part of the essence of technology is "calculative thought" in Heidegger's sense, then the digital clock is an enhancement of this process.

Clocks were, prior to the rise of science proper, part of the daily experience of Medieval humanity. They were an ordinary part of the lifeworld, the technological mediators of the sense and perception of time. And in a sense, they made possible the very calculations which lay at the much later basis of measurement undertaken by the Galileos and Keplers of the early scientific era.

Turn now to a spatially mediated experience and note that the same invariants occur again. One of the most important technologies which allowed the science of the modern era to become truly experimental was optics. Lenses were developed in the tenth century, were already compounded by the thirteenth century, and simultaneously with the first explicit scientific observations, the microscope and telescope were invented.

Vision is embodied and mediated through lenses. What changes is what might be called a shift of focus from ordinary perception to the technologically mediated micro-dimension. Distance is reduced, what is far is brought near, but this is equivalent to saying that what was for ordinary vision a micro-feature is now made present. The microscope brings into view for the first time the small and unexpected creatures found in drinking water; the telescope reveals that the shaded areas of the moon are seas and mountains and craters. The span of space is changed, reduced, and the object is "brought closer." What was previously so distant as to be unperceived, is now perceived in a near-distance of optically mediated space. Again, both what is focal and what was the field of space changes under the transformations of technologically mediated perception.

This is to say, that through the use of technologies, experience had already become prepared for the scientific experience of the world. A world whose features could be considered as discrete units, a world whose micro-features would fascinate, a world conceived of under the sign of mechanical relations, was a world which was prepared for by the taken-for-granted technologically mediated experience of the Medieval Period.

Late Medieval experience of both time and space could be considered to be thoroughly embedded in and often mediated through technologies. One could expand upon these examples in many areas of life. One could also contrast these examples of technologically mediated perceptions of space and time with cultures which did not have clocks or lenses and note that time and space are differently perceived by the latter. But I shall now turn to a more dramatic example of the way experience and praxis are organized and examine a crucial case of long-distance spatial orientation, the variant development of a perceptual and technologically mediated perceptual navigational system.

B. Variant Long-Distance Spatial Orientation: Atlantic and Pacific Navigation

One of the features which stimulated the European development of technology, was the availability of ideas and devices from many areas of the world, an availability made possible through the early exploratory trips of Europeans. We are familiar with some of the historical events which were associated with this cross-cultural interchange: the Crusades, the travels of Marco Polo, the centuries of coastal voyages; and only much later, the full spice trade and voyages of conquest for gold and riches which fed the end of the Medieval Period. I shall focus here upon the development of cross-oceanic navigation as it contrasts with the Pacific variant.

Coastal navigation, essentially navigation within sight of land or never far from it, is distinctly different from transoceanic navigation. The principles or practice of coastal navigation and the body of knowledge which goes with it were known from ancient times. Such navigation was largely perceptual and traditional since observations of currents, animal life, noise and sight of breakers over shoal waters, wind patterns, etc., were necessary for safe coastal piloting. Fears of out-of-sight navigation were not merely those clothed with superstitions about the unknown (monsters, the end of the world, etc.) but were related to a lack of knowledge about how to return to a known area. In short, what was needed was a means of dependable spatial orientation across the expanse of uncharted ocean.

Early Western transoceanic navigation was successfully undertaken by the Vikings who traveled from Scandanavia, not only throughout Europe and the Near East in coastal raids, but also to Iceland, Greenland and Nova Scotia in the New World. How these voyages were undertaken lies somewhat obscured by a sparse historical record, except that we know that two features of navigation unique to Northern Europe were already known: a fixed star, the North Star (Polaris) was known and navigational calculations could be based upon this fixed point. And the primitive use of the lodestone which also points to a fixed area, was already common with the Vikings. Thus, although very simple, one can say that the very origin of transatlantic navigation was technological in a most primitive sense. Orientation was secured through a device.

If, however, one takes the voyages of Columbus as more typical, then the technological determination of orientation is abundantly clear. By 1492, the transition period for our purposes, not only is there a magnetic compass, but measured and careful cartography was known, and a more vast array of instrumentation was also available. Compass, astrolabe for calculating angles to the sun and other heavenly bodies, clocks (although not yet fully useful for ocean voyages) and various measuring devices were used for navigation. Columbus's daring voyage was a voyage undertaken through a technologically mediated orientation to possible space. (Columbus knew very well that the earth was round; that it was of approximately a certain size—although vastly underestimated by his era—and that it could be plotted through calculations via instruments.) His navigation already conceived of the world as a grid upon whose surface one moved, and his perceptions were instrumentally mediated. Thus our earliest voyages through the period of world exploration were voyages which were undertaken through technologies.

When one turns to the Pacific we find that the Polynesians and related peoples had, already 1000 years before the Vikings, explored and populated virtually every inhabitable island chain of a much larger ocean. Western explorers were amazed by the 200-foot-long catamaran war canoes which speedily navigated the Pacific, yet they did not pick up the secrets of Polynesian navigation at the time. One must conclude, on the basis of praxis, that both Atlantic and Pacific navigation were successful, but on examination, each was a distinct and different system.

Polynesian navigation was instrumentless; it operated without fixed points such as Polaris, which is not visible in the Southern hemisphere; nor did the Polynesians have the technological fixed point of the compass. It was a rather complex system of perceptual observations carried on through a secret tradition by a school of navigators.[21] I shall not outline all of the features of this perceptual system, but shall point to enough features to illustrate its subtlety:

(i) One key feature of the perceptual system was a highly developed sense of wave patterns. Waves march with regularity across the Pacific and the Polynesian navigators learned to use them for precise directional purposes. By judging the angle of swells in relation to the direction their canoes took, Polynesian navigators could maintain direction. They became so keenly aware of this wave harmonic that even when local storms confused the seas, they could detect the swell pattern engendered by the storm. (Often they would sit in the bottom of the canoe to feel this pattern—their claim was that only men could navigate so because they felt the pattern in their testicles). They also were aware of what we would call refraction waves: swell patterns bend when they approach a land mass such as an island and the change in direction was detected and understood as an indication of a distant island.

(ii) Cloud and light patterns were also learned. Far over the horizon a column of cloud, slightly green tinted skies, and other

The Historical-Ontological Priority of Technology over Science

more dense moisture indications would be read as the presence of an island. Again the indications were perceptual readings of the phenomena.

(iii) Although bird behavior and patterns were not unknown to European coastal navigators, the precision of observation which knew exactly how far each species strayed from land, the knowledge that a direction towards land could be obtained at dusk by returning birds, and even knowledge of which fish inhabited near-island waters enabled the Polynesian navigators to regard the ocean stretches as a familiar, readable world.

(iv) Star paths were learned and conveyed from generation to generation of navigators. Lacking an immovable pole star, the Polynesians developed a highly temporal, dynamic mode of reading star tracks over the horizon with changes of direction timed to moving locations. Indeed, all constants were in effect dynamic and temporally changing constants in this system.

Here was a navigational system which historically was at least equally successful in conquering transoceanic distances, a system which had more difficult tasks to perform since small island systems are harder to locate than continental masses, and a system which was thoroughly perceptual and historical. It was a system whose "map" of the earth was based upon perceptually acute readings of the ocean, without either a mathematics except for a time since (but no clocks) or an instrumentation. It was a variant orientational praxis.

One might very well expect that a variant praxis would be sedimented in a variant understanding of the world; and that certainly is the case. The Polynesian view was—if interpreted by Western standards—"animistic." The ocean was not perceived as either alien or strange, although its dangers and threats were clearly appreciated. It was a deity whose many natures could nevertheless be understood. It was the source of nurture and support and thus a voyage upon its face, while it may pose dangers, was not a voyage into the wild nor something over which humans could expect mastery.

Do not misunderstand the point I am making here: I am not claiming that this life-world is better than that of the technologically oriented Modern. But it is different. Its praxis, focused perceptually, achieves similar goals although it implicates a different understanding of the world. It is a world which does not become standing-reserve because the earth's bounties are conceived of differently.

One might also point out that the Polynesian world is one which is disappearing. Its navigational arts, though still extant among a small number of persons, have been replaced by the now highly micro-determined instrumented navigation of the West. Long voyages by islanders are now undertaken on trading schooners or ships. (Although their ability to sense land before the Westerner remains, trading schooner captains indicate that they have lapsed into only rough navigation because they know that their passengers will begin to sing when approaching their island, long before the Western captain knows it's near.) My point is that two differently patterned praxes implicate two different ways of understanding the world, and ours is and has been historically Technological for centuries, indeed virtually for at least a millennium.

If Heidegger is right, that the essence of Technology shows itself only recently, it is because we have failed to look at what was under our very noses for a long time. But Technology is like a set of spectacles: those who see through them and who have become accustomed to them, do not notice them. Thus that which is closest and most familiar to us, we have failed to notice. Yet what we have failed to notice turns out to be basic, perhaps the most basic thing about the very way in which we see the world.

V. Conclusion

I have suggested that there is a significant sense in which Technology is both historically and ontologically prior to science. This priority, I believe, is one which is not contrary to the more trivial sense in which the human use of technologies is both universal and archaic, common to all cultures whether or not they have developed science.

I have also suggested that the way in which this priority operates is at the level of a basic praxis within a life-world, a praxis which inclines or predisposes us towards what becomes a scientific world view. I have developed only some of its features—those which include a technologically mediated basic perceptual experience. This is an experience which harbors invariant characteristics such as transformed foci regarding ordinary and microdimensions of experience, a tendency towards discreteness and the atomization of things, and the enhancement of calculative activities. In this sense Technology at the level of familiar praxis precedes and sets the conditions for a science.

Science, in turn, becomes the coming to self-consciousness of these activities, a self-consciousness which both projects the form of life implicit in the praxis upon the universe, and a self-consciousness which becomes increasingly purified of diverse elements. Such a purification, however, is also a purification of the essence of Technology.

Even the Renaissance, enamoured of inventions, and its desire to measure and use the world, created its artifacts in the form of animal and human life. Da Fortana's measuring robots were conceived of in the form of fish, rabbits and birds. The predecessor of the steam boiler was the *sufflator*, literally "blower," whose shape was always that of a human head whose mouth blew forth the steam which powered various devices. Only gradually did the *abstraction* needed for contemporary Technology emerge, thus freeing technologies to be "scientific" as embodiments of a purely technological metaphysics.

The gradual movement to de-animate our technologies, to move towards purer *functionalism*, is both latent within technology and a preparation for a scientific world view. It is a long step from the symbolism of the clock whose movements represented the heavenly bodies to the bare, instantaneous numbers of the digital, but the movement is one towards a more totally technological and scientific representation.

There is one question still left unanswered in this chapter, the issue which separates idealist from materialist interpretations of science and technology. But it may begin to be understood in a different way, too. That issue is whether or not and in what sense *scientific* technology may be distinctly different from traditional technology. My answer is that in one sense it is different, in another not.

The sense in which it is not different is the sense in which technologies have and continue to have the same existential dimensions with respect to the humans who use them. Technologies may embody and mediate experience so that our life-world undergoes changes; technologies may be "other" than we as that to which we relate; and technologies may increasingly be surrounding features of our life-world. In each case these appearances of technology may be seen to be continuous with even the most archaic technology.[22]

The sense in which scientific technology differs from traditional technologies depends upon the synergistic interaction of a technology made abstract or purified through the self-consciousness connected with science. Thus the break from "natural" materials to the manipulation and creation of materials, the gestalts which occur between scientific fields, and the extrapolations made possible by revolutions in science could only happen when the essence of Technology has become manifest. But precisely because it has become so, we can now notice more distinctly and clearly that we are wearing eyeglasses, and we can begin to reflect upon the implications of that wearing.

CHAPTER THREE
The Technological Embodiment of Media

I. Introduction

The simplest and purest notion of a communication relation between individuals would be one which might be characterized as a "face-to-face" relation. It would be akin to John Dewey's notion of the simplest school, two individuals seated each on the end of a log, conversing with one another uninterrupted and unimpeded. A simple dialogue between two individuals exemplifies such a communication situation.

In such a situation, whatever complexities, might arise, would arise with respect to the speakers themselves. Thus clear, honest and straightforward communication could still be impeded if one or the other speaker should dissemble, lie, exaggerate or utilize any of the many possible devices humans use to hide from or fool each other. But at the same time, the face-to-face situation is one which allows for the condition of the possibility of authentic, truthful and open communication.

What happens, then, when this direct communication situation is varied such that the situation is no longer that of two individuals seated on their respective log ends, when the communication must take place through some third element, a medium? Factually and familiarly this second situation is one which is more and more commonplace and which is simply taken for granted by most of us in advanced technological society. What day does not go by without the use of the telephone—a common medium? Or in which we do not listen to the radio or television for anything from entertainment to getting vital news and information? Or when do we not pick up a newspaper, magazine or book as yet another genre of taken-for-granted media?

That communication occurs by means of media is such a commonplace that we rarely reflect, let alone reflect critically, upon the implication of what I shall call a "third factor" in the communication situation. We are, furthermore, quite aware that all of the possibilities of distortion which can occur in the "face-to-face" situation can also occur with the use of media. Lies, dissembling, covering over things, are just as possible with media as they are with humans face to face. And because this is so in a rather obvious way, we might be tempted to simply assume that everything which is possible in the face-to-face situation occurs in a "mediated" situation—and in some sense it does. But we might also be tempted in this assumption to overlook a whole dimension of interesting phenomena which are unique to the "mediated" communication situation.

The theme for this investigation is what role do media play in the situation of human communication? Does the introduction of such "third factors" as media change or transform the communication situation? And, if so, how? My inquiry, then, is *a phenomenology of media* with particular focus upon the experience of media in concrete communication situations. My general argument is one which will seek to demonstrate that there is a unique way in which the introduction of media—communications technologies—transforms the communication situation. This transformation of the communication situation, I shall argue, is both inevitable (a necessary condition) and nonneutral (transformational) with respect to any communication situation which utilizes communications technologies. A phenomenology, as an inquiry into these phenomena, directs itself to uncovering what might be called invariant or essential features of such situations, and in the process begins to unravel somewhat broader implications for the human impact of technology overall.

To accomplish this task I shall take the following steps: (a) First, I shall examine some of our usual ways of looking at things, including the ways we often overlook important features of our experience of things. What might be called the impact of communications technologies upon human experience is often simply overlooked, and often, if not overlooked, might not be isolated with sufficient clarity to merit its own investigation. (b) Second, I shall introduce in brief and simple terms some of the key phenomenological notions which I shall employ in undertaking exactly such a thematic study of the communications situation. And (c) third, I shall then proceed to analyse a series of common media-embodied communications situations to point up and isolate the specifically invariant features of the technological transformation of human communications.

II. Technologies of Communication

First, I shall take a brief look at certain temptations we have which cause us to overlook the unique effects of technologies upon our communication experience. What has become known as the electric communications revolution began earlier in the century. Older media, such as print in all of its forms, have been with us for some centuries, but the newer media, embodied in electronics technologies, began to allow the human voice itself to be carried to distances never possible for even the most imaginable shouting match. One such early invention was the transatlantic telephone cable. With it Edison's Watson was able to be heard not just in a nearby room, but across the ocean. But problems emerged: the very machinery which was to transmit the sound of the voice created its own noise which was also transmitted. Indeed, after certain distances, the noise of the machinery (amplifiers and the like) was such that it literally "covered over" the sound of the voice which was supposed to be transmitted. Here, one could clearly claim, the technology being employed was nonneutral in an obviously negative sense. It intruded into the very purpose of the system, to convey an understandable human speech. Something had to be done to impede the machinery-produced noise and to enhance the desired sound, that of the voice, if the communication were to occur at all. This is to say, the transmission must *embody* the conversation "transparently" and not itself intrude into the communication situation.

We, of course, now know the outcome of this early communications technology problem. We can now telephone practically anyone in far-reaching places of the world and hear them as clearly as, or better than, the earlier technologies allowed us to hear persons in the next village. (We have even replaced the cable with satellite today.) Experientially this is to say that some degree of hoped for "transparency" of communication has been achieved. While not all noise of transmission has been removed, it is now no more than background to the foreground of technologically mediated human speech.

In this example, however, the nonneutrality of technology as it embodies human communication, has been noted negatively. Insofar as transmission noises intrude into the mediated communication situation, they impede and restrict that communication. This apparent negativity, however, can also be inverted as in the famous example developed by Martin Heidegger in his analysis of our use of equipment, specifically tools. His example was the use of a simple hammer. The user of a hammer, he points out, does not focus upon or relate *to* the hammer in the work situation at all. Rather, when the hammer is functioning in the use situation, it is the work—that upon which the human using the hammer works—that is experienced. In such situations the hammer "withdraws" or becomes "transparent" as the very condition of its usefulness. This is a positive feature in the use of a technology which allows us to perform otherwise unperformable tasks. Similarly, when we make a long-distance telephone call, the instrument and its associated and very complex equipment experientially "recedes" and we simply focus upon and experience the conversation with the other. In short, when the technology is good—at least in this kind of use situation—it becomes semi-transparent with respect to communication. It can be functionally "forgotten." Conversely, only when it functions poorly or doesn't work at all does it obtrude itself into our experiential aims. A measure of the quality of this type of technology is in fact the degree of "transparency" which it may allow the user.

The extension of this observation for communication situations is clear enough—those media which most enhance "transparency" will be seen in some sense to be superior to those which obtrude into the communication situation. The clear-sounding telephone system which allows me to recognize the individual voice of the other is obviously superior to one which makes the other sound so "phony" and "tinny" that he or she is a mere generalized other. And if this degree of auditory transparency is best when maximized, can we not anticipate even more adequate forms of more global transparencies? Should we not move towards the television-telephone where we could see as well as hear the other? I shall return to this later, but at the moment I wish to take account of two temptations which pose themselves at precisely this juncture of the inquiry.

We have now recognized that for a technology to function well, it must itself become a kind of barely noticed background effect. It must itself "withdraw" so that the human action which is embodied through the technology can stand out. This "withdrawal" or "transparency," however, simultaneously poses us with two temptations which can make us forget certain essential features of the mediated communications situation.

First, if the better the technology is the more it becomes transparent, couldn't we hope for and aim towards what I shall call the *perfectly transparent* situation? Could we not have a technology which was so perfect that we couldn't notice it at all? This is what I shall call the idealization of a technology. Note two interesting aspects to this temptation: first, what would the perfectly transparent technology allow? Obviously, a nonmediated communications situation, one in which the technology was so transparent that it would be invisible and thus *equivalent* to being a nontechnologically mediated situation. In short, this is an idealized reduction to the simplest communications situation, the face-to-face situation which is itself *not* technologically mediated.

The dreamer who wishes for the perfectly transparent technology thus secretly harbors a wish for no technology at all—or at least its equivalent. The dreamer would like to be face-to-face with the other. But this does not occur with actual technologies, because no matter how relatively transparent they become, they remain far from perfect transparency. But what I am pointing out here is what I regard as a deep ambivalence in the idealizer: there is simultaneously a wish *for* certain things which a technology can give us, for example, the long-distance communication which the long-distance telephone gives us, *and* a wish that the technological embodiment be functionally nontechnological or direct. In short, this is something like a wish to be godlike.

If the first temptation is one which opens a direction toward the idealization of technological possibilities, the second temptation is one which allows us to *forget* the subtle presence of a technology as a "third element" in mediated communications situations.

A "good" technology, we have seen, does not call attention to itself, it "withdraws" in use. And the better it functions, the more likely it becomes that we may simply grow used to its functions and "forget" that it is there and that it is a significant element in our new mediated communication situation. We take the technology for granted in such a way that we increasingly disregard its presence. In this, we allow whatever is unique to the mediated communication situation to be forgotten or covered over. But what if the use of a technology, *any* technology, is essentially nonneutral? What if such uses transform human experience and communications in fundamental ways? Should we not then become precisely aware of and reflective about such transformations? Put positively, should we not attempt to reflect critically and deeply, precisely about the ways in which we communicate in such technologically embodied situations?

It is at this juncture that I wish to turn to a more analytic description and begin to develop a phenomenology of communications technologies.

III. A Phenomenology

I begin by very briefly and simply taking note of a few major conclusions phenomenologists have drawn about the shape of human experience. I then move directly into an elementary application of these notions to a simple communications situation before moving to more complex variations.

The key notion used by phenomenologists to interpret experience is called *intentionality*. This term contains a multiplicity of meanings, but designates primarily a certain "shape" of experience. What is claimed is that all human experience is *directed*—it is selective and focused upon an experienced environment which we shall call *world*. A world is an experiential space and time which is simultaneously present to us and yet in some sense "other than" and "distant" from us. I shall formalize this first characterization of intentionality thusly:

$$\text{Human} \longrightarrow \text{World}$$

Here the "human" is the experiencer and the "world" is that environment which is experienced. The arrow signifies the involved focus of experience as it is directed towards "world." What we have here, then, is a primitive theory of action—I am primarily a being who acts towards and within a world (and action in the phenomenological sense includes even *perceptual* acts; indeed, in some sense these are basic.)

This directed, actional involvement with a world is not only one-directional, however, it is also reflexive or interactive. Phenomenology interprets intentionality as not only a distance from and involvement in world, but as *reflexive* with respect to world. This is to say that the shape of our experience is such that, at bottom, what we eventually come to know of ourselves is strictly reciprocal with what we come to know of the world. Without world there would be no self; without self, no experience of world. The reflexive structure of intentionality, then, can be signified by noting the way in which world is taken back into my self-experience with a second arrow making intentionality interactive:

$$\text{Human} \xleftarrow{\quad\quad} \dashrightarrow \text{World}$$

These illustrations point up a minimal set of operative notions from phenomenology which can now be applied to the inquiry into the experience of media. What remains is to isolate and delimit the inquiry so as to detect the salient features of the transformations of experience which media make possible. In doing so I wish to introduce a technical interpretation of what shall count as a medium for purposes of this essay: A medium, as I shall use it here, will include (a) some material artifact which is experientially used in a particular way to (b) convey what may be called broadly an expressive activity. Thus the ordinary sense of media, such as newspapers, radio, cinema, television, will be preserved as in each case there is an artifact or set of artifacts (technologies) which are used to convey information, messages, entertain, stimulate or arouse.

Such media may be said, in normative use, to *embody* expressive activity and to embody it by means of some *materialization* which may include word, image, action, reproduction, representation or whatever. I shall exclude from my notion of media the ordinary, though somewhat strange usage of an art form as a medium. Someone who performs a dance *is* performing and expressing; the dance *is* the expression and thus I will not consider the dance to be a "medium." Instead, a medium will necessarily be something which is between the expressor of the expressive activity and the recipient just as the spiritualist medium is presumably "between" the living and the dead. By being situated between the direct expressive activity and the recipient a medium inherently occupies a potentially *hermeneutic* role. (The hermeneut is an interpreter, for example the priest or oracle who conveys the messages of the gods.)

By so defining the media-situation—a definition which I think will be seen to be appropriate to the phenomenon—I also may relate media to the phenomenological understanding of intentionality. The nonmediated situation may be symbolized as follows:

$$\text{Human} \longleftrightarrow \text{World}$$

In this symbolization the intentional interaction with the world may be described as *direct*. What I have in mind are what I have called earlier *face-to-face* situations. Here normal human dialogue

The Technological Embodiment of Media

may be taken as the paradigm. When you and I speak face-to-face our mutual experience is directed towards each other. The perceptual situation is such that the full play of the senses is open—I see your gestures, hear your intonations, feel your expressive presence, etc. Such a situation is unmediated. Thus in such situations I shall not speak of media.

If, however, I were to speak to you over a telephone, the situation is dramatically altered. In this case the dialogue is not face-to-face, but mediated by means of the telephone. The telephone as a medium is *between* us. This may be symbolized with respect to intentionality thusly:

Human ——————— medium ——————➤World.
(I ——————— telephone ——————➤you)

What this formalism takes account of is a medium in *mediating position*. The artifact (telephone) is taken into intentionality and occupies a mediating position.

First, note that the medium of the telephone is such that it may be said to embody the dialogue; it makes your voice present to me and mine to you. In so doing the artifact when functioning well "withdraws" or becomes semitransparent as noted. At optimum function, I am able to recognize your voice as yours and although your presence to me is *reduced* perceptually to a mere voice, the presence is one in "real space-time." This capacity of a medium to materialize us to each other in spite of vast geographical distances, is, of course, one of the advantages of media. I shall call this advantage the *ampliflicatory dimension* of media. A medium makes something possible either in a sense of enhancing an ordinary possibility—for example, the megaphone enhances the volume of the voice so that it carries farther and louder than ordinarily. Or in a more radical sense, a medium provides the condition of possibility for something not before possible—the transatlantic telephone carries the voice to distances simply not possible in any face-to-face situation. But at the same time the advantage is gained at a price. Your presence to me through the telephone is—compared to global perception—a reduced presence and laking in the perceptual richness of the face-to-face situation.

I shall call this the *reductive dimension* of a medium. This is to say that simultaneous with—and inextricably bound to the amplificatory dimension (which is usually regarded positively)—is the reductive dimension which subtracts something from the richness of ordinary global experience. I am here illustrating this structural characteristic of media by what happens perceptually.

It is together that this amplification-reduction makes a medium nonneutral or transformative of human experience. It is, moreover, a feature of every use of a technology. Please note in passing that the term, nonneutrality, is carefully chosen in such a way as to preclude either some immediate "good" or equally immediate "bad" connotation for technologies. It is rather *essentially* or invariably *ambiguous*. Precisely because this ambiguity is inescapable, it makes the use and development of technologies simultaneously fascinating, threatening and in need of serious reflection.

Not only does a technology contain an invariantly transformational factor, but it does so in a specific way. Every technology has what I shall call a telos, or weighted center of gravity which makes it partially selective as to what may be enhanced and what reduced.

In the example of the telephone, if all I need is information, the telephone seems relatively adequate; but if you are an intimate, while the immediacy of the telephone is better than the more "abstract" letter, there remains a sense of lack. (Here imaginative compensations may occur to fill in the experience, but in contrast to the possibility of genuine face-to-face contact these remain only a partial satisfaction.) Here we begin to sense what might be called a center of gravity to a given medium, a center which is only relatively adequate to some purposes and less so with respect to others.

And even if the telephone permits genuine embodiment of a real space-time dialogue, it does not do so without transforming that dialogue. The space-time of a telephone conversation has a certain *irreal* character to it as well. For example, the space-time of such a conversation is always that of a *near distance*. This distance is neither geographical, in the sense of having a clear perception of far and near, nor the distance of normal life space as in dialogue space. It is rather the mediated space-time in which all distances are made quasi-near (I can hear you just about as well from the next town as from California or even Europe—if the technology is good), but equivalently you are never perceptually fully present and thus you remain simultaneously irreally distant. In short, the medium transforms the other and the situation in which the other is made present. This transformation is *nonneutral*.

So far, I have taken a familiar situation and begun to unravel its effects within normal experiences. Familiarity often covers over what may be noted to be quite striking effects. We do not think twice about telephones, yet they dramatically transform the possibility of human dialogue by making it possible in situations never before available, as well as making it possible by transforming the very meaning of the presence and location of the other.

The telephone is a mono-sensed medium and thus is a partial sensory experience. This partiality is, moreover, ambiguous. Its familiar mediation is such that we now have habitual patterns of telephone relations which we take for granted. There is currently much experimentation with an audio-visual form of communication, a television-phone. The ambiguity of our habit is pointed up by the mixed response to such a device—some think it would be nice to be able to see the other as well as talk to him or her, while others, on second thought, note that they might well be caught without their pajamas. There are both advantages and disadvantages to the partiality. This is to say that the telephone as a medium has been taken into daily life in a certain way, and we organize our very communication patterns around the peculiar capacities of this instrumental embodiment. Such effects are subtle and precisely because they are so familiar, we may fail to take note of the way in which our very experience of the other has been transformed.

A more complex medium—let us take television—displays the

same essential features. Although the television is bisensory (audio-visual) it remains both an extension of our sensory experience in space-time and a reduction of that experience. In this instance the transformation of space-time may be quite dramatic, so much so that the "live" performance is the exception to the general practice of replay in which the immediate life-world reference may no longer even exist. I only too well recall the somewhat ghoulish anticigarette commercial in which a recently dead actor had pretaped his moral not to smoke. He indicated that he would be dead of lung cancer when seen on television. The television brings what was past and that which is or was elsewhere into the near-distance of the media *now*. In this sense it reenforces our experience of an irreal presence of mediated otherness. The quasi-abstract character of the television image remains untouchable and distant while simultaneously being present here and now. But what stands forth as the focal phenomenon is the pervasive presence of the mediated now, the near-distance of what is heard and viewed.

The extension-reduction of media has another facet as well. In format, contemporary television (at least in capitalist countries) differentiates little between the 7 o'clock news and Walt Disney. A report on deaths in some world revolution could just as well be interrupted by a commercial as could segments of a cartoon feature. But the point here is not a diatribe against commercialism; it is rather the observation that space-time in the medium takes on a certain disjunctive character. The medium has as a capacity a technological "transcendence" over ordinary space-time. The freedom of control possible in editing and constructing a program is closer to the reverie, to the imaginative dimension than to ordinary life. (This is obviously not to extol the current "imaginativeness" of television!) It has, therefore, the same tempting power as the more ancient medium—print—for those who wish to escape from tedium, boredom and the ordinary. The viewer may escape into the reproduced reverie just as the reader of pulp novels may do.

I do not intend, in this characterization, to suggest that escape is the only possibility of media such as print or television. On the contrary, the extension which is possible to a wider world of humanity, nature, or whatever is also a possibility. What I am suggesting, however, is that the extension is of a particular kind, an extension which simultaneously reduces, amplifies and transforms the referent to some particular *mediated* presence.

The media world is thus a transformed world. Note that I am not saying that it is either merely an imitation of or reproduction of the ordinary perceptual world. But I am saying that it is a variant "world." So far the level of analysis has only varied between direct perceptual situations in which no media are positioned and mediated perceptual situations in which media occupy some position between the experiencer and the referent of the experience. However, there is a complication which enters this situation. The mediated perceptual situation remains in a basic sense perceptual. I am the one who sees the television, who hears the voices. And while the presumed ultimate referent is somewhere else, I also immediately perceive the television presence. This is to make the obvious point that all experiences has its perceptually basic dimension, but it is also to point to something else. Insofar as the medium is immediately experienced, it also transforms the larger perceptual situation. Indeed, media become part of the total perceptual situation. And if at the first level one may detect the irreal dimension of a mediated perception, at a second level one can also claim that this mediation has now been materialized and thus becomes part of reality. This is, of course, to say that media have a "real" effect.

At this level the real effect of media has certain implications for the way in which we interpret our overall experience. I shall describe this effect by a series of gradations whereby initial analogies which are taken to be metaphorical gradually become so common they are taken literally. For example, in much psychological description, particularly in description of the experience of subjects, it is now common to talk about imagination, memory, dreams and other image-related experiences as being "like" a movie. At this stage we have a clear example of cross-sorting in which there are obvious analogies between two distinctly different phenomena. In fact, the similarities rather than the differences, tend to get emphasized although the differences may be as important as the similarities.

Such cross-sorting has often become so traditional that it becomes assumed that the likeness is virtually identical. In a first cross-sorting approximation, the similarities are merely noted and distinctions glossed over. Life becomes "like" the movies just as movies may be lifelike. (Many persons remark that it seems as if they have "seen this movie before" or report that they feel like they have "been in this movie before.")

Noted that in this cross-sorting, causal relations or relations of origination may work in either direction. Certainly prior to the experience of movies and television, imagination and memory would not have been described as "movielike." Rather, imaginers and rememberers inverted the process and often deliberately modeled their sequences upon imaginations and memories (as did literature before). But once having become part of the life-world, the dream-imagined-remembered sequences now materialized become part of the way in which we come to understand ourselves and our world.

At the other end of the process of cross-sorting in which a metaphorical relation becomes understood as nonmetaphorical, one can also discern a relation to media-induced experience. In recent years I have attended a number of interdisciplinary conferences dealing with computer technology and artificial intelligence. To my constant amazement I find that there are always a number of participants (usually mathematicians and highly theoretically oriented computer programmers) who take the human mind and the computer not to be metaphorically similar, but (potentially) literally identical. Here the process of cross-sorting has lost its suggestive analogical basis and become a metaphysics. But this phenomenon should be expected by a phenomenologist. If it is the case that intentionality is genuinely interactive between world and self; and if that "world" increasingly becomes encapsulated or at least focused upon some narrow set of intriguing phenomena; then at least for the noncritical and reductively predisposed mind it becomes almost inevitable that "I" will become "like" my experienced "world."

I am suggesting that a technological world is not only one in which we are increasingly related to the media, but also one where relations may be nonneutral in at least two important senses. I have shown how the transformation of basic perceptual experience occus in the experience of media; and now I have suggested that at the level of human self-interpretation the experience of media becomes pervasive and familiar and begins to inform our ways of understanding ourselves. While I suggest that this effect is pervasive and subtle (and it is not linear, for single items or developments would be hard, if not impossible, to detect), it is an effect which is hard to demonstrate globally.

A global effect can probably only be hinted at speculatively. I shall conclude this foray into media by suggesting one such possible global effect. At the more micro-analytic level of a phenomenological analysis of the telephone, I suggested that the medium of the telephone transformed our usual perceptual sense of space-time into what I termed an irreal near-distance. I would contend that this feature is in fact invariant in experienced media and is enhanced by the more complex media such as film or television. But as we experience such media not only more frequently but also more dominantly, we gradually become so familiar and habituated to this way of relating to the world that the initially sharp variation between the media world and the nonmedia world becomes less distinct. This, in turn, allows the condition of the possibility of transformed space-time to be increasingly taken as "real" space-time.

What would such a space-time be? In part the answer is approximately a near-distant space-time in which all "spaces" and "times" are made quasi-near. That this is a media capacity is clear. Kennedy's assassination, Vietnam, even the news hour replays of old newsreels, complemented by the fictional futuresque movies of "Starwars," etc., bring such "spaces" and "times" into the Now. *But*, while media space-time has the possibility of making near, it does so always at a distance, a distance which *reduces* the perceptual or fully lived sense of the phenomenon. The media-phenomenon is *hermeneutic*—it is mediated. Its presence is that distant presence which needs the adumbration of critical imagination to "come alive."

Once again the analogy to that now ancient medium, print,

emerges. The new media have capacities which writing has always had—but with a difference. Precisely as the medium approximates perceptual experience (the cinema brings the action before one, one does not have to imagine it), it becomes ever more difficult to be a mere observer. Instead, the near distant space-time of media has as a center of gravity on the part of the viewer, a viewing which is something like an "aesthetic stance."

An aesthetic stance in this speculation is a stance which is *between* what could be called "observer consciousness" and direct actional involvement. Again a series of graded examples can show the weighted form of viewing which is implied. A viewing which is primarily that of observer consciousness is a detached viewing, the kind of viewing we ordinarily associate with the highly perceptive but personally distinct viewing of an experiment. Such a viewing, to be sure, implies a discipline to be constituted and implies a subterranean commitment to certain ideals such as those entailed in scientific enterprises. At the other end of the continuum would be direct actional involvement such as we find in the normal affairs of daily life. With friends, family, and colleagues our engagements are primarily actional. But with the speculative aesthetic stance implied in the media experience, we find both a distance and an involvement of a peculiar sort. Cinema and television do not call for immediate action—the bumpkin who jumps on the stage to slug the villain in a melodrama would be the counterxample to an appropriate distance in media viewing. But neither does the expressive activity presented through media leave us without engagement. It engages the wider spectrum of our experience including our emotional life, but it engages it in the near-distance of a drama-like situation.

Once again this analysis of contemporary media calls forth reflections of long-familiar experience, the experiences of reading, literature and the performing arts, each of which entices a variation of an aesthetic stance for our response. But what is different in the contemporary use of media is not only the extent of media use which virtually permeates much contemporary life, but the same enticement towards an aesthetic stance in daily life. Cinema and television are still primarily entertainment devices or information devices which most often use situations appropriate for the aesthetic stance. But telephones, the increasing use of other communications media and even the communications uses of television-mediated interpersonal engagements bring this stance into the vicinity of action.

The larger and even more speculative question which arises from this observation can be hinted at both by way of an open conclusion and a suggestive question: Does the daily experience of media incline though not determine our experience of others increasingly towards a shaped world which reflects the essential possibilities of media? In other words, does the near-distance which is essential to the experience of media; does the possibility of the disjunction in space-time; does the very concept of "role" now analogous to dramatic play incline us towards a particular form of social life? Were we to observe that contemporary life reflected this pattern in terms of human relations in which roles are significantly and frequently shifted, in which any person potentially could be a "relationship," in which discontinuities were taken to be as normal as continuities, we might have food for thought regarding the more global impact of media upon our form of life.

CHAPTER FOUR
Why Do Humans Think They Are Machines?

The question I should like to deal with in this chapter is: why do some humans understand themselves to be machines? Indeed, how can they conceive of themselves in this way? *That* they so interpret themselves as machines or at least machinelike would seem to be clear and commonplace enough. We easily and readily accept such notions as machine-body counterparts such that we do not think twice when our hearts are referred to as "pumps," our skeletal and muscular systems as "levers," or our eyes as "cameras."

Such cross-sorting of simile and metaphor between our bodies and machines is, of course, hardly new. It has been a commonplace at least since the rise and victory of Modern Philosophy, particularly as expressed by Descartes who observed that animal—and by extension—human bodies could be thought of as "cleverly contrived machines." Today, however, the machinelike qualities of the body have carried over into the philosophy of mind such that we have also begun to think of our mental states—our thinking—as machinelike. Those who are intrigued by both artificial intelligence and cognitive simulation speak as if, and some seem to seriously believe that, our minds are "cleverly contrived computers."

My purpose in taking up this question will not be to determine whether or not we are indeed "cleverly contrived machines." In fact, I think that dealing with this question at this level necessarily begs important questions and hides within it such deep ambiguities that it probably can't be simply unraveled. Instead, I wish to look below the surface of the question at a somewhat

Technics

broader phenomenon, the phenomenon of human self-interpretation. What makes it existentially possible for humans to ask: am I indeed a machine? or in what ways am I machinelike?

The stance I shall take in dealing with our penchant to interpret ourselves as machines couples two unlikely philosophical bedfellows: Martin Heidegger and David Hume whose ideas have been touched upon in chapter two. What I wish to draw from each is the following: Heidegger's most influential philosophical work is *Being and Time*. There he sought to develop a fundamental analysis of human existence, which he called our *being-here* which is his suggestive literalization of the ordinary German term for existence, *Dasein*. His most general assertion which opens this inquiry into human existence is the observation that humans are beings who in some way in their very relationship to the world necessarily also interpret themselves. Human existents are those beings who interpret or understand themselves. This is the way he puts it in the introduction:

> Dasein is an entity which does not just occur among other entities. Rather it is ontically distinguished by the fact that, in its very Being, that Being is an issue for it. But in that case, this is a constitutive state of Dasein's Being . . . And this means further that there is some way in which Dasein understands itself in its Being, and that to some degree it does so explicitly. It is peculiar to this entity that with and through its Being, this Being is disclosed to it. Understanding of Being is itself a definite characteristic of Dasein's Being.[1]

Now, if I may paraphrase this into non-Heideggerese, what is being said is this: Humans are those beings who in the act of existing are concerned for and ask after existence. In so doing, this is not only a characteristic of them as existents, but the way in which this activity is engaged in necessarily entails understanding or *interpretation*. In short, humans cannot escape self-interpretation; it is a characteristic of their being.

I shall accept this general assertion, that humans are beings who necessarily interpret themselves and I shall look at this general existential phenomenon as instantiated specifically in the contemporary penchant towards a particular self-interpretation, namely, the machinelike self-conception of some human beings. And I shall ask both why they so interpret themselves and how they might come to such a conclusion at this point in history and time.

My second philosophical bedfellow is David Hume, whose *Dialogues Concerning Natural Religion* contain a discussion highly relevant to the question of human self-interpretation. In these dialogues Hume inquires into certain tendencies regarding human attempts to define and describe God or God-interpretations. Specifically, he develops an argument against the use of analogies to adequately describe God, analogies which he finds to be misleading and fallacious as the basis for many of the so-called arguments for the existence of God.

I wish to do two things with these arguments. First, I shall look at the most salient points Hume makes regarding the misapplications of analogical reasoning as a prelude to relating these same arguments to the contemporary penchant to regard oneself as a machine, and secondly, in this redirection of the Humean arguments I am taking the points he makes concerning the limitations of God-interpretation to be equally valid for human-interpretation. In short, although God arguments may often today be thought to be antiquated, human self-interpretation may not be so antiquated.

In Hume's *Dialogues*, Philo, who speaks for Hume, notes:

> . . . All inferences concerning fact, are founded on experience and all experimental reasonings are founded on the supposition that similar causes prove similar effects and similar effects similar causes. . . . Unless the cases be exactly similar, they repose no perfect confidence in applying their past observation to any particular phenomenon. Every alteration of circumstances occasions a doubt concerning the event; and it requires new experiments to prove certainly, that the new circumstances are of no moment or importance. . . . The slow and deliberate steps of philosophers here if anywhere are distinguished from the precipitate march of the vulgar, who, hurried on by the smallest similitures are incapable of all discernment or consideration.[2]

In short, we have a rigorous standard applied to any argument from metaphor or analogy. Furthermore, any argument which extrapolates from some partial analogy to either a total analogy or even an identity makes the mistake of taking a part for the whole.

Hume, entering into an argument against taking some aspect of the universe for the whole in the argument for God from design, notes:

> Thought, design, intelligence, such as we discover in men and other animals, is no more than *one* of the springs and principles of the universe, as well as heat or cold, attraction or repulsion, and a hundred others, which fall under daily observation. It is an active cause, by which some particular parts of nature, we find, produce alterations on other parts. But can a conclusion, with any propriety, be transferred from parts to the whole? Does not the great disproportion bar all comparison and inference?[3]

Then, applying this rigorous criterion to the arguments concerning God, Philo argues that Cleanthes, is guilty of anthropomorphism concerning the partial similarity within the universe as a whole with some human attributes:

> But to show you still more inconveniences . . . in your anthropomorphism; please take a new survey of your principles. Like effects prove like causes. This is the experimental argument; and this, you say too, is the sole theological argument. Now it is certain that the liker the effects are, which are seen, and the liker the cause which is inferred, the stronger is the argument. Every departure on either side diminished the probability, and renders the experiment less conclusive.[4]

Now, having set the criteria which affirm the necessity of strict likenesses for affirming identity, and having taken note of the fallacy of taking a part for a whole and of projecting anthropomorphic features upon the whole, Hume then does a nice *reductio ad absurdum* on arguments from analogy. Take initial note of how he does this from historical examples.

First, he argues that were any argument from analogy to be valid, any other likely analogy would in effect be as good as any other. He proceeds to trot out several examples—which I shall call cultural variations in phenomenological fashion. His first example is: Why not consider the universe to be the body of God; it is more like a functioning body than like an artifact which was designed:

> Now if we survey the universe, so far as it falls under our knowledge, it bears a great resemblance to an animal or organized body, it seems actuated with a like principle of life and motion. A continual circulation of matter in it produces no disorder; a continual waste in every part is incessantly repaired; the closest sympathy is perceived throughout the entire system: and each part or member, in performing its proper offices, operates both to its own preservation and to that of the whole. The world, therefore, I infer, is an animal, and the Deity is the soul of the world, actuating it and actuated by it.[5]

Obviously, ultimately this example must fall under the same critique as the example of the world as the grand designed artifice of a Creator because the analogy is partial, and inference is made from some small resemblance to a total identification. Hume goes on to press the reductio by then noting that another likely analogy can be found in likening the universe to vegetable growth, "if the universe bears a greater likeness to animal bodies and to vegetables, than to the works of human art, it is more probable that its cause resembles the cause of the former than that of the latter, and its origin ought rather to be ascribed to generation or vegetation than to reason or design."[6] And, finally, in pressing the equivalence of analogies, Hume notes that in certain possible circumstances it is equally conceivable to think of the universe as arising from the bowels of a great spider after his version of the Brahmin myth. He concludes, "Why an orderly system may not be spun from the belly as well as from the brain, it will be difficult . . . to give a satisfactory reason."[7]

If Hume is right concerning the illicitness of making inference about totalities from parts and about the need for recognizing the possible fallacies lurking in any argument from analogy, his arguments would in principle bear upon any critique of humans interpreting themselves as machines. However "like" machines they may or may not be, there remains enough disanalogy to foreclose any *identification* of humans with machines. At most there may be a partial likeness in certain limited respects and like Hume's vulgar thinker who has not yet reasoned slowly and piecemean to rigorous understanding, we merely find ourselves in the midst of the new "theologians" who go about arguing that we are indeed machines.

My purpose, however, is not to directly attack the machine analogy—were it that, I think Hume's arguments remain telling—but rather to attempt to account for the recalcitrance of the analogy. This must be done by turning to the sources of self-interpretation.

I have, so far then, two themes from related but rarely paired bedfellows regarding self-interpretation. On the one side, I have Heidegger's observation that humans cannot escape some either explicit or at least implicit self-interpretation. In describing and interrogating the world itself, we find ourselves included in such a way that we cannot avoid self-interpretation. On the other side, if we accept Hume's critique of analogical reasoning, we find that there are traps in self-interpretation such that we are likely to be led astray by the various metaphors and analogies we develop to interpret ourselves.

I may now begin to dig more deeply into the general phenomenon of human self-interpretation with its specific tendency to take a mechanistic turn in our era and culture. First, we need to get some sense of distance to our often taken for granted analogy of human-machine likeness by repeating the Humean strategy of noting other likely analogies. I shall consider these minimal phenomenological variations. In phenomenology, however, variations are used to reveal *invariant structures* and what I am after is something like a structure of self-interpretation.

Now were we modern Humeans, we might well begin by noting that there are clearly competing historical and cultural examples of analogies regarding humans. Historically it should be clear that humans have not always conceived of themselves as machines. And they certainly have not taken such an interpretation either for granted or dominantly. Prior to the rise of Modern Philosophy in the seventeenth and eighteenth centuries it might seem that the dominant metaphor of self-interpretation was the *imago-dei*, the human existent as the imitation of or reflection of God. And if one wished to know what that meant then one must know who or what God is. That this should prove to be a difficult task does not surprise us nearly so much as it actually exercised the best minds of the Medieval period. And while I shall not examine the arguments which emerged during this time, I do wish to make a general observation upon the way in which the structure of the interpretation presented itself. Human self-interpretation was taken to be modeled upon something "Other" than itelf, in this case the godhead. It was by means of God that humanity attempted to understand itself. Self-understanding was modeled upon the understanding of something 'other.'

If this first historical variant shows us that our dominant version of self-interpretation was not always the case, or phenomenologically put, if there are other viable alternatives or variations, a brief turn to anthropology makes such variations even more dramatic. For example, one highly frequent metaphor of self-interpretation in nonindustrialized peoples is an animal metaphor (again recalling Hume). Humans are thought to be like, related to or be kin of various kinds of animals (and here we must add that animals are thought of quite differently than we think of them now. They are thought to be certain kinds of spirits with certain kinds of characteristics, clearly not mechanistic ones.) In other societies the vegetable kingdom and its annual cycles constitute the primary pattern of reality which is reflected in humankind. The cycles of birth, growth and maturation, fruition and death, repeated by birth determines the model upon which and from which humans seek to understand themselves. Indeed, we have something like the progression of Hume's metaphors here—why not think of God-qua-humanity as "spiderlike" or "vegetablelike" or as "designerlike"? But the point here is initially a minimal but strong one. There are variants such that we cannot claim that one such variant is sufficiently self-evident or superior without some associated defense. And it may turn out that none of these variants are sufficient for deeper reasons than have appeared so far. This, then, is a small first step at distancing ourselves critically from particular versions or instances of such interpretations.

But we may also begin to note something else about these examples. In each case the analogy grasps its likeness by pointing to something which is "other" than human to interpret what is human. Does this same thing happen in the contemporary case of the human-machine metaphor?

Clearly there is a sense in which the machine is "other," but in the case of this analogy the "other" is curious. Our previous examples were in some sense natural examples. Analogies to animals, to vegetative cycles or even to gods have a base in nature in a broad sense. With machines, however, something else gets introduced. Were we merely to distance ourselves from our familiarity with machines for a bit we might well begin to see that this is strange.

There is clearly a rigorous sense in which we can claim that before and prior to humans there were no such things as machines. Machines are artifacts which are conceived of, developed and invented, *made* by humans. And were we to use a creator-created relationship to describe this genesis of machines, we would clearly identify the god with humanity and the creation with the machine. Yet, when we look at the current situation in which humans increasingly understand themselves to be machine-like or even to *be* machines, we find that something like an inversion has occurred. The god in this case has taken to interpreting itself through its own *imago*. There remains, however, a structural invariance with the previous examples. Something which is "other" —although in this case the otherness is an otherness which is created by the one who interprets—is the machine which gets reflected back upon and into its creator.

It is at this point that I may be more explicitly phenomenological to explicate what may be happening. There are three theses which may be combined to help account for the prevalence and depth of the metaphor of the machine which so dominates contemporary self-interpretation.

The first thesis may now be called the *existential thesis*. Humans are, in some sense, what they do. Each era and culture takes a variant shape, a *praxis,* which builds a life form. Take the simple case of eating. The dominant polite form of eating in Western societies employs a technology of knives, forks and spoons. This practice is sedimented in an order, purpose and arrangement whereas many Eastern societies use chopsticks and bowls in an equally sedimented fashion. In addition there are nontechnological modes of grasping food which include the bare use of hands and fingers (including our fast food habits).

In recent times there has appeared a wider and wider set of activities which involve technologies in Western industrial society—a life form which I shall characterize as *technologically textured.* So dominant is this embeddedness of human-technology interfacing that from waking (alarm clocks, etc.) to toilet activities (whole systems of water and sewerage) to eating (microwaves) to virtually every activity (including the technology of sex) there is technological involvement. This texture becomes the dominant, familiar and taken-for-granted activity of this "world" of human inhabitants. Put simply, this technological texture forms one reason for the dominance and recalcitrance of the metaphor of the machine in that our familiar world is simply ordinarily technological.

Technologies in the daily experience of humans, of course, are not new. But the degree and extent of the texture is. No Western navigator (save for the rebel) would dream of long-distance navigation without instruments, whereas traditional Polynesian navigators simply did not dream of using instruments. Even our most extreme encounters with nature are technologically mediated. Mountain climbing in the contemporary sense is made possible through stainless steel pitons, artificially produced boots, dacron-braided ropes and the like. Wherever we turn, our relations to others, the environment and ourselves are embedded in a technological texture.

The second thesis may be called the *otherness thesis.* I have noted that whenever human self-interpretation occurs, an invariant feature seems to be that we interpret ourselves by means of some "other." Here is a deep root of the metaphor. At other times and places, humans interpreted themselves, as Hume rightly noted, by means of vegetable, animal or other human or divine means. An other is chosen as relevant to humanness and the insights developed therefrom are reflexively internalized as a metaphorical self-interpretation. In this sense our penchant to self-interpret by way of the machine metaphor is functionally equivalent to the most primitive reflexive self-interpretations. Our deanimated or mechanized "world" is internalized in a fashion not different from the way archaic humans reflected their more animistic (familiar to them) "world." We become "like" our "world" in the same way that they did theirs.

In the contemporary jargon of some psychology, it is not far from possible to mistake the descriptions of human behavior in textbooks as virtually identical with descriptions of wiring diagrams for space modules. Indeed, the current uses of "hard" and "soft wiring" metaphors as descriptions of human behavior possibilities seem deliberately to suggest such close analogues. One might multiply the examples: we project "biological clocks" into animals, ourselves and even insects (although the "clock" was projected into the heavens long ago). Our "otherness" is the machine and by means of it we establish the twentieth-century "likenesses" between our familiar technologically textured world and ourselves.

If, on one level, machine otherness functions identically with other self-interpretative otherness (animal, vegetable, etc.), on another it would seem to be different. In a narrow sense there simply were no machines before humans invented them. Humans were the "gods" who created machines, perhaps in their likeness, but who then found themselves modeled upon their own artifacts. Thus one can note the curious inversion which occurs with this form of otherness. The creator interprets himself through the created.

A second thought, however, reveals that this projection and reflection is not so different from archaic otherness. What strikes us as naïveté in primitive thought is its obvious anthropomorphic quality. In each society in which animal metaphors are dominant one finds animals classed and described as not only animallike, but as having qualities shared with or like humans. The coyote is cunning, the owl wise, the lion brave, thus the analogical projection is easy to reflect. Although it may seem on the surface that such anthropomorphic naïveté is a leap from the present, only our familiar involvement keeps us from seeing that the same anthropomorphism occurs in our current obsession with artificial intelligence at least as a metaphorical projection-reflection. Our dominant metaphysics has long selected, out of the whole range of thought phenomena, calculations and logical operations as not only the most important dimensions of thought, but as central to thought. We build computers to imitate such thought and then reflexively believe that we are learning something of our own thinking. Not only is this metaphorical move reductive (mistaking in Humean fashion a part for the whole), but it overlooks the equally striking dissimilarities.

The computer is no more (or less) like the mind at work than a building crane is like a human arm. It does something "better" (calculates faster and if programmed correctly with less calculational error) and other things worse or not at all (it can't devise totally alternative strategies, consider contexts, or a whole series of other quite ordinary mental operations) just as the crane clearly amplifies the power of lifting and strength far beyond that of the human arm but would be hard put to pick up a needle or tickle a pussycat. Yet we no longer are fascinated, as was the early industrial era, with the mere amplification of human muscle power. In fact, a case could be made that until the mystique of the metaphor is broken, it might well be impossible for us to develop the unique otherness of machine capacity for its own possibilities. I am suggesting that so long as this mystique of the metaphor reigns in artificial intelligence that we remain on the level of design seen early in the use of gothic frillery on locomotives (pretty, but irrelevant). There is probably more to be learned and done by exploring the dissimilarities than the similarities.

The third thesis is the deepest and most subtle one. I shall call it the *interpretative thesis*. It is here that I shall return to

Heidegger, after having reaped some suggestions based upon Hume's insights. What Hume's critique does is to give us a devastating set of arguments for showing what is not or should not be the case for understanding human self-interpretation. No single set of metaphors can be adequate, nor should they be reified, because doing so inevitably reduces the richness which is humanity. But what Hume's negative arguments leave out is the sense of what or where the unique characteristic of humanity may lie. Just as Hume, without a self-reflective turn, could find no self (Husserl's criticism), so without a similar self-reflective turn one is doomed to a procession of metaphors and thus Humean skepticism.

But if one does take a self-reflective turn, based upon the first two theses regarding praxis and otherness, then one finds that there is one human action which opens the way to a nonreductive understanding of humanity. That activity is interpretation itself.

Humans, whether archaic or contemporarily scientific, undertake interpretation. Interpretation, reflexively self-interpretation, is an essential aspect of human being. This was Heidegger's insight. And interpretation in its very nature outstrips any particular metaphorical reification. Interpretation is "transcendence." But interpretation as a phenomenon often remains hidden.

The hiddenness of interpretation can easily be seen by returning to the contemporary penchant for taking the metaphor of the machine literally. The psychologist who describes human behavior as "hard wired" in some form as if the subject were a mechanon, is himself or herself *doing* an interpretation. Indeed, were "hard wiring" to apply self-reflexively to the act of the psychologist's as if it were itself such a "hard wired" phenomenon, the result would quite correctly be described as a short circuit. Interpretation transcends the psychological explanation just as the psychologist transcends the object of his or her description. Yet, to admit this would be to admit that a mechanistic theory itself is inadequate and thus the act of interpretation within the theory is kept repressed.

Interpretation, however, as an act is contentless. It must *refer* in order to be an interpretation and this reference is what calls for some kind of otherness. Interpretation is interpretation of _____. If interpretation is a clue to human transcendence, it is so by virtue of being so paradoxically. Its index is an indication of human openness to possibilities, but openness to possibilities may be fulfilled only by filling that openness specifically. The analogy or metaphor, in this sense, returns as a kind of necessity made necessary by the act of interpretation itself.

We are thus situated paradoxically in trying to grasp self-interpretation in that, on the one hand, we are necessarily interpreting beings, while, on the other, in the instant of interpretation we find in its fulfillment a reduction of the possibilities of interpretation. To say everything is to say nothing, but to say something is never to say enough.

We thus remain caught in a tension between Hume and Heidegger. Were we to eschew analogy altogether, would we be able to say anything? Is Humean skepticism the silent answer to Hume's critique? And yet to say something, even through the weakness of analogy, do we not imply more, at least implicitly. Any saying is to interpret, which is potentially and implicitly to have already transcended the metaphor. Something like this lies behind Heidegger's enigmatic view of technology itself. Only by seeing *through* technology can we see where and what it is. And only by seeing through our penchant to interpret ourselves as machines will be able to find out who we are.

PART TWO
Perception

CHAPTER FIVE

Phenomenological Variations and Artistic Discovery*

If philosophy is an essentially *rational* mode of thinking in which the predominant patterns of thought are or can become systematic concerns, it should be expected that such phenomena as innovation, invention, discovery and the whole realm of the genuinely creative would pose a problem for philosophers. Such phenomena contain, at the least, elements of surprise, novelty, serendipity, and at most may appear unprecedented and unpredictable.

In fact, philosophers have devised a number of strategies or tactics of explanation in the face of creative or novel phenomena. At one extreme they may accept the existence of such phenomena as genuine, but relegate this existence to a realm at best indirectly related to rationality. Theories which see discovery as basically irrational, arbitrary, or eruptions from dark or Dionysian undergrounds, give creativity its own realm, but place it just beyond the reach of rationality.

The other extreme in effect ultimately denies the essentially surprising aspects of creativity and subsumes them into an ultimate inevitability of a systematic logic. Such tactics try to find ways to show that what is taken as novel, was in fact, virtually inevitable. Thus a Monet, whether or not instantiated by the Frenchman named Claude, would have occurred sooner or later anyway with the combination of new theories of light in painting. This strategy sees novelty as an epiphenomen of a pervasive necessity which is the model of its rationality.

---

*Paper delivered to the British Society for Aesthetics, University College, London, September 25, 1977.

Both of the above strategies presuppose some separation between what may be called a systematic rationality and the real or apparent irruption of the creative. Thus the human activities which are called "philosophy" and "art" are often separated. This division which contains an ancient prejudice, goes back at least as far as Plato who characterizes artists as doing what they do by some form of intuition without system or self-knowledge. Such a division of activities is, in fact, institutionalized in our civilization.

In this chapter I should like to suggest that such a division and prejudice is neither beneficial to philosophy nor to art and to offer what might be called a third tactic, the tactic of *systematic discovery* in which certain qualities of creativity are taken into the very model of rationality itself. I shall suggest that the phenomenological method offers just such a possibility. Specifically, I wish to show that what phenomenologists call the "intuition of essences" and their method of "phenomenological (fantasy) variations" constitutes a kind of "logic of discovery."

This thesis may be caricatured by observing that the very model of phenomenological rationality is essentially "artful." And, contrarily, it may be said that the arts are at the least latently "phenomenological."

Although the bulk of this chapter will be a demonstration of how variational method (fantasy variation) may be employed systematically, it may also be noted from a philosophical point of view that the arts actually exercise the practice of variational discovery. Through the possible the actual is revealed.

In the arts the characters in a novel are "possible" people; the steps of a dance are, at least in relation and in contrast to more mundane movements of our bodies, "possible" movements; and the plays of form, figure, light and color are variations of the possible in visual art. Thus one might say in this respect that the arts are latently "phenomenological" in their primary use of variations.

Contrarily for philosophy, I am in a sense accepting what is often given as a criticism of phenomenology—that it is, or at least is *like*, an art. The often derrogatory "phenomenology belongs to poetry" is, in part, correct. But with Aristotle, whose claim is that poetry contains a greater truth than history, I will try to show that this kinship is beneficial for an emergent concept of philosophical rationality and possibly beneficial for the artist who learns from the rationality of phenomenology.

The core of my argument will be by way of exemplification. I shall take a single set of examples which were worked out in my recent book *Experimental Phenomenology* (Putnam's, 1977) to show how phenomenology operates, to illustrate and exemplify what I see to be a core for a systematic "logic of discovery" which is both related to and relevant for artistic activity. But while I shall not here outline anything like a full scheme of phenomenological method, it is necessary to point to the two related phenomenological concepts which give rise to this systematic use of variational discovery.

The two concepts are those already referred to as (a) the intuition of essences and (b) the use of a variational method. And although all phenomenologists use variants upon these concepts, my context today will be roughly Husserlian. In this brief expository section I shall merely try to show how these two concepts relate to one another and show how a certain operational result begins to appear.

The intuition of essences (or structures) in the broadest sense, is part of a phenomenological theory of evidence. It has two parameters for purposes here. The first parameter is what may be called "empirical" in the sense that for an essence to be intuited *it must be fulfilled or fulfillable in actual experience.* Although it may be fulfilled in any number of ways (perceptually, imaginatively, volitionally, etc.) its presence is what counts, within the limits of how it is presented, as intuited. A remark is perhaps relevant here with respect to Husserl: the Husserlian paradigm is basically a mathematical one. What may be called "intuitional demonstrations" are analogous to mathematical demonstrations. The insight into a solution "fulfills" the perplexity initially posed by a problem. When all the parts fall together, when the equation is solved, one has "intuited the essence" in the Husserlian sense. In this context, fulfillability now becomes a criterion of evidence.

Thus for purposes here, the intuition of essences will be broadly seen as a goal of investigation. An intuition is fulfilled when, and only when the phenomenon becomes present in some way to actual experience. And although the qualification that the mode of its presence is equally important to note, for our purposes I shall concentrate upon the fulfillability of a given set of phenomena.

The second concept is primarily a functional one. Variational method is a means of seeking, and hopefully finding what is fulfillable. It, too, is broadly "empirical" in that actual investigations are undertaken to see what can be discovered about any particular phenomenon. Once again it should be pointed out that in the original Husserlian context the implicit paradigm continued to be a logical-mathematical one. Prior to the actual solution to a logical or mathematical problem, various routes might be attempted. And in many instances, even given a solution, one might find variant ways to reach the same conclusion. It was this use of variations which Husserl, for the most part, had in mind.

However, he also wished to broaden this paradigm into all areas of experience, thus variations were in his case thought of as possibilities for other dimensions of experience than the conceptual. There could be perceptual variations, conceptual variations, imaginative variations, etc. And at this earliest stage he already saw the possibility of a relationship to what might broadly be conceived of as artistic activity:

> Much can be drawn from examples furnished by history and, even more by art and especially literature. Undoubtedly these are fictitious; but the originality in the invention of forms, the richness of detail, the continuous development of motif raise them high above the creations of our own imaginations.[1]

Nevertheless, it is also fair to indicate that Husserl himself did not take this advice, but relied upon his own very mundane imagination. His own examples are far from imaginative and were drawn from the most common items so dear to philosophers: trees, desks, inkstands and the like.

From the whole range of possible variations, however, Husserl did raise one type of variation to at least functional primacy. These were alternately called "imaginative" or "fantasy" variations. There were two practical reasons for elevation of fantasy variations given: (i) Imaginative activity was thought by Husserl to be able to replicate any other activity, particularly perceptual activity. (ii) Because this "mere imagination" could be substituted for other modes of activity, one could also go through variations rapidly, easily, and while at one's desk—a favored position for the philosopher in contrast to the anthropologist or artist—and thus could serve as a kind of shortcut to more laborious trials and errors in other dimensions. Philosophers rarely do field work.

I, myself, think both of these reasons insufficient and think the first observation to be, in fact, phenomenologically false, but the point here is to indicate how even in its Husserlian beginnings, phenomenology elevated imaginative activity to its core importance. Imaginative variations became the primary means of seeking fulfillment of essences and the two concepts remained fundamentally related. "Freedom in the investigation of essences necessarily requires that one operate on the plane of the imagination,"[2] Husserl claimed.

We have, now, two closely related concepts: (a) the intuition of essences as the goal of inquiry with fulfillment as evidence, and (b) variational method by which the essence is to be discovered. I have claimed that this activity is both systematic and imaginative and that it constitutes a core for a logic of phenomenological discovery. Naturally, these two notions are not sufficient to stand by themselves. They take their place in a more elaborate methodological context which includes the whole theory of phenomenological reductions—but I shall stick to my pledge not to elaborate this whole framework for purposes here. Instead, I shall now turn directly to what might be called an "intuitional demonstration" of how these concepts work in an actual phenomenology of a limited set of examples.

It is probably appropriate, in comparing artistic activity and phenomenology, that the examples are visual ones. I shall not claim great artistic merit for the figures about to be presented—they are line drawings which you will all recognize immediately—

but they can serve as a set of highly simplified examples of an artistic phenomenon. This very simplification will help to stimulate the investigation. The drawings are what are known in psychology as the Necker Cube series. I begin with the most common example:

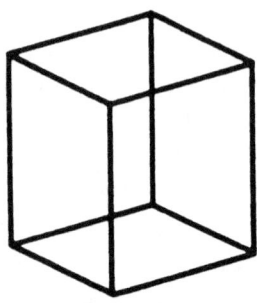

Here we have a common two-dimensional drawing of a three-dimensional cube and it is ordinarily taken just as that. There is, however, one strange thing about this ordinary representation of a cube—in psychologist's language, it reverses itself. That is, it may be seen in two ways, either as a cube "facing forward" as it were, or as a cube "facing rearward" and these two aspects seem to spontaneously reverse themselves.

In my phenomenological context I shall call each of these appearances perceptual *variations* and name each. Thus the forward facing variation will be $3d^f$ and the rearward facing variation, $3d^r$. At this juncture I note that (1) each variation is equally possible, (2) that each is mutually exclusive, they alternate but do not combine, (3) that each is genuinely intuitable in that I can and do experience each variation. Thus both $3d^f$ and $3d^r$ may be called genuine or essential possibilities of the drawing.

Here we have a primitive and simple example of a beginning phenomenological analysis of a simple phenomenon. Essential aspects of the phenomenon have been discovered and at least two variations have been noted as the first way in which the intuition of essences and variational method are combined. But to this point we have also remained within the realm of the ordinary—what

Husserl would have called the "natural attitude"—and remained content with what is already sedimented or what constitutes the common.

Is this all there is to it? Clearly, the demonstration achieves what Husserl called "apodicticity" in that the two fulfillments are certain, and are present within experience. But is this *adequate*? (Here I must recognize in passing that the wider context of theory will be presupposed in the following steps.) In an essential, as contrasted with a merely factual science, possibility precedes and exceeds factuality. Husserl's theory of phenomenological reductions are but elaborate ways of seeking an *adequate* intuition of the essential. Thus behind the core investigative tool, variational method, is the implicit rule: *seek all possible variations,* not merely those which first meet the eye. It is this heuristic aim which imports the latent logic of discovery into variational method. It is that which remains unsatisfied with either the ordinary or the surface aspects of a phenomenon.

Thus, returning to the cube, I now ask: do variations $3d^f$ and $3d^r$ *exhaust* the possible variations of the figure? I now move from the "natural attitude" into a "phenomenological attitude" in purposely seeking all possible variations upon the figure. But while this seems a radical move, I also still remain under the stricture that if the essential is to be discovered, it also must be genuinely intuitable, made present in my experience. Are there other (perceptual) variations for the cube? This move may be facilitated by a device. Technically, what I am about to do is part of the process of "bracketing" in that I set aside my ordinary assumptions to seek the purely essential, but I have found that heuristically an imaginative aid speeds up the process. Thus in the next variations I shall import a brief "story," a hermeneutic device, although through a longer and more labored analysis I could show the same things without the story.

I return to the drawing, and this time instead of remaining satisfied with accepting it as a cube, I seek other variants. Suppose the first of these is as a non-three-dimensional possibility. Suppose that the drawing isn't of a cube at all, but is of a rather odd shaped insect in a hexagonally shaped hole. In this case the central aspect of the drawing is his body; the lines which connect this body with the perimeter are his legs; and the perimeter itself is the outline of the hole within which he is situated.

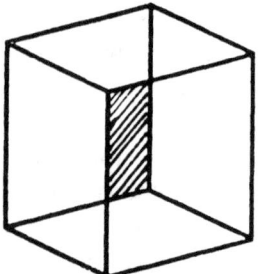 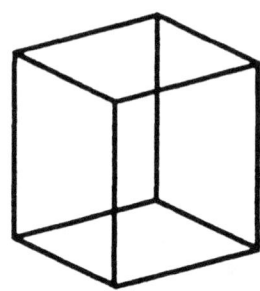

A moment usually suffices, but then this new and now two-dimensional variation takes shape. Stepping back into our analytic position, we now have *three* variations which may be symbolized as: $3d^f/3d^r$ and 2-d. With but little practice the intuitional fulfillment of the 2-d variation becomes easily attained. If, now, I return to the three characteristics previously noted, I again discern that (1) each variation is possible (although for the moment it may seem that variation 2-d is "more difficult"); (2) each is mutually exclusive in alternations, and (3) each is genuinely intuitable, fulfillable, or apodictic. But I may now add a new or phenomenological characteristic: (4) by breaking with the ordinary appearances I have expanded the variational possibilities such that the ordinary appearances now take on a new significance. They remain apodictic, but apodicticity now becomes somewhat weaker in comparison to the newly opened field of greater possibility. Apodicticity is relative to adequacy. But adequacy is now open; I do not yet know if I have exhausted the variational possibilities of the drawing. However, I have opened the way toward an ideal limit. The "meaning" of the first appearances changes in weight.

Once again I return to the drawing, again with the phenomenological attitude, and seek additional variations. To speed the process up, I again revert to a story: suppose that the figure is neither a cube nor an insect in a hole, but is an oddly cut gem.

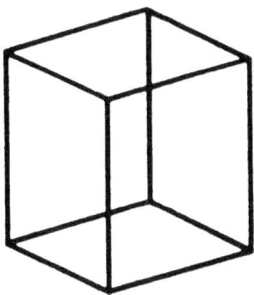

In this case the central configuration is a facet of the gem. Suppose the gem is lying in a case and this facet is uppermost and facing the viewer. Then the other facets (lines which connect with the perimeter) are sloping downward or away from the viewer, and the perimeter is the outside limit of the gem. Again, this variation, perhaps initially even more difficult than the 2-d variation, does reach a gestalt and is intuited or fulfilled experientially.

When this occurs, we have not only a fourth variation upon the drawing, but a new three-dimensional variation. In our analytic series we now have $3d^f$, $3d^r$, and now $3d^{f'}$. Those who are rapidly now catching up in this analysis will probably have already attained an anticipatory insight which is already an essential insight: if the first 3-d appearance was reversible as a genuine variational possibility of the drawing, might we not expect the second to be reversible as well? The answer is "yes." Return once more to the gem variation, but this time the viewer is "inside" the gem looking outward. In this case the center facet is facing away (rather than near) the viewer and the outward facets are sloping towards the viewer. This variation yields a second 3-d variation and the fifth in the series of variation: $3d^f/3d^r/2-d/3d^{f'}/3d^{r'}$.

By now one may begin to see a whole new series of questions emerge. Some obvious ones are: how far does the series of variations extend? Is the extension finite, indefinite, infinite? Is there some privilege to the "ordinary variations," or are these merely arbitrary, that is, could the series be constituted in any order at all? What roles do imagination and perception play, respectively, in this process?

Within the limits of this paper I shall not deal with all of these, but I do wish to point to two phenomenological gains which should have emerged in the demonstration to this point: (1) The use of variational method, impelled by the implicit telos of the phenomenological reductions, opens up the sense of phenomena. Specifically, it opens the sense of phenomena to essential levels, that is, the level of structured possibility. (2) As this level begins to take shape—as it is just beginning to do in this example— the essential analysis begins to look more and more like a topography. A topography is a mapping of the structure of possibilities, not just of first or ordinary appearances.

But, indirectly in the process something else occurs. That is what may be called the phenomenological education of experience, in this case perceptual experience. It is this education which may inform artistic activity. And it is this indirect result which I wish to help solidify in the remainder of this paper. Thus, rather than pushing the analysis further, I wish to reinforce it by repeating it in two other cube drawings:

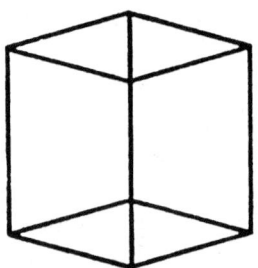

This drawing is a variant upon the Necker Cube, but it is usually still taken as a cube. The constitution of the first two variants is easy, once again: $3d^f$ is seen as one variation and $3d^r$ as the other. But we are now also in a new position vis-à-vis this drawing. Phenomenologically we already suspect that there are other possibilities and we are no longer "naïve" subjects or viewers.

For fun, constitute a slightly different order for the remaining variants. If this drawing has the same essential possibilities as the first, we should already suspect that a second set of three-dimensional aspects is possible. An anecdote allows these variants to take shape: Suppose that this is not a cube, but that the viewer is inside a church looking upward at the inside of the roof. The central line is the ridge pole or far vertex of the roof with the lines leading downward toward the perimeter which is where the walls would meet the bottom of the roof. Thus we have $3d^{'}$. A reversal is simple: Suppose the viewer is in a helicopter above the church, now the roof ridge is facing the viewer with the sides of the roof sloping downward for $3d^{f'}$. In the new series we now have two sets of three-dimensional variants, synonymous with those of the first cube drawing, but they have also occurred in a different order: $3d^{f}/3d^{r}/3d^{r'}/3d^{f'}$ with the 2-d variant not yet constituted (which one should be able to do for oneself at any time). We thus have the same five possibilities rather than the original two, and as we consolidate the investigation, we may begin to see that these variations are, at least in principle, "equally" possible as essential possibilities of the drawing, indeed of the series so far.

Even more rapidly, allow one final example in my series:

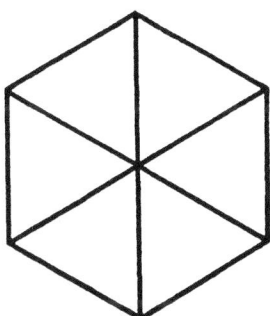

This cube variant is the last in my series and once again I wish to point to the same five variants in succession, but again in a different order than either of the previous examples. In this case —were one not already aware that the drawing is a possible cube—it might be the case that its 2-d appearance would empirically occur first. It is a hexagon with lines leading to its center for variation 2-d.

This time, let us locate the noncube three-dimensional variants first: Suppose one is lying on one's back inside an American Indian's teepee, looking upward. The vertex is where the poles come together; the lines are the poles sloping downward to the juncture of ground and the bottom of the teepee. We have, then, variation $3d^{r'}$. For a reversal, we take the same helicopter outside and above for the near vertex variation and $3d^{f'}$.

Finally, we return this drawing to its place in the Necker Cube series and reconstitute it as a reversible cube with a near variant, $3d^f$, and a far variant, $3d^r$. Thus we have constituted the five variants now demonstrated as possible for each of the drawings in the cube series. The essential possibilities are seen to belong to each to the same extent.

We have now taken each of the three drawings, presumably each variants upon a cube, and phenomenologically begun to *deconstruct* them by means of variation. In this demonstration I have remained content to take the same five variants from each of the drawings. This intuitionally (or experientially) begins to demonstrate something about the essential features of such ambiguous or multi-stable configurations. First, recalling our criteria, the demonstration shows that (1) each variation is possible, (2) each is distinct and mutually exclusive, and (3) each is fulfillable and thus apodictic. But in the process, itself a very simple instance of a logic of discovery in action, other insights and new questions also emerged: (4) the initial phenomenon, at first restricted to an ordinary context, was opened to new possibilities or variants. The phenomenon was shown to contain *more* than it was first taken to contain. This indicates both that there is more complexity or richness to the phenomenon than initially expected and that there is more to our awareness of how such phenomena can be taken. (5) There is here an implicit ascendance in level by the move from a "natural attitude" to a "phenomenological attitude" which deliberately seeks variations within all phenomena. (6) What began to show itself through variational method is something like a topography of such phenomena, a topography which would

Phenomenological Variations and Artistic Discovery

have remained unsuspected except for the intuitional demonstration of the variations.

In other words, this topography is something like a depth structure when compared to the surface structure revealed within the limits of the ordinary view. And with the appearance of a depth structure, new problems emerge. Take note of only one such problem: Is there a "natural" order of variant appearances? Or is the other arbitrary? And if "natural," why and how is this order constituted? The demonstration suggests these questions itself.

A chart may illustrate the constellation which now is revealed concerning the cube series:

		$3d^f$	$3d^r$	2-d	$3d^{f'}$	$3d^{r'}$
Cube #1	Variant					
	Order	1	2	3	4	5
Cube #2	Variant	$3d^f$	$3d^r$	2-d	$3d^{f'}$	$3d^{r'}$
	Order	1	2	5	3	4
Cube #3	Variant	$3d^f$	$3d^r$	2-d	$3d^{f'}$	$3d^{r'}$
	Order	4	5	1	3	2

Although the same variations occur in each drawing, the order is different. This suggests that at some level the order is arbitrary. That is, once the move is made to an essential rather than "empirical" or ordinary level, the order could appear in any way within the series. Here, I suggest, there is something like a non-transitive move from the "natural attitude" to a "phenomenological attitude" brought about by the use of variational method. Once it is discerned that there is a depth structure to such drawings it becomes no longer possible to remain merely satisfied with the surface features of a phenomenon. In this concrete case, once a multi-stable abstract figure is seen to contain a series of possibilities, while the first or ordinary appearances may at any time be recovered and fulfilled, they are also seen to belong to a larger series of possibilities, the series of which has its own structure.

It is this movement from what is sedimented or the "natural attitude" to the level of possibility that the "phenomenological attitude" refers. In classical terms it is the move from mere opinion to genuine science.

This conversion of insight, however, never loses what was previously taken as ordinary (although it transforms its significance). The apodicticity of the first variants remains repeatable and certain. However, it must take a new position within the essential science as but one possible variation among others. And even if this position should be shown to be privileged in some way, the position is no longer absolute nor isolated. The ordinary must take its place within a wider field of possibilities.

This is as far as I will go here with the partial phenomenological analysis I have been demonstrating. It is bifurcated, partial and perhaps at best suggestive. But I would like to conclude with a few speculative remarks concerning phenomenology and artistic activity.

I have been implicitly demonstrating something like the free rein of the imagination which Husserl suggests is necessary for phenomenology. I think I need not do more than refer to the obvious when I suggest that at the core of artistic activity is also a need for a free imagination. But I would like to suggest more: the phenomenologist's move to essential variations is deeply analogous to the moves from the ordinary attitudes which are constantly exhibited by the arts. In dance, for example, were there not something like both a possibilizing attitude toward human bodily motion and the development of a topography of those possibilities, dance would have forever remained at best a copy of walking, jumping and rolling about. Instead, dance has broken beyond the bounds of such copying to instantiate moves which take us to the very limits of human bodily motion. Anyone who has seen Nureyev perform one of his spectacular leaps which seem to defy the very laws of gravity with the pause which occurs at its apogee, knows of what I speak. Likewise, the novelist, while usually retaining a core of believability for characters, pushes us into the possible states of being human which frequently occur in novels but rarely in mundane life. Artistic activity, I suggest, is necessarily quasi-phenomenological in this sense.

If artistic activity is always quasi-phenomenological in the sense of exhibiting possibilities within a field, at this level of generalization artistic activity could remain limited to Platonic naïveté. This is to say that artists could practice or discover variations without a logic of discovery, for it is clear that much artistic discovery works in just such serendipitous ways. But I would like to suggest that in contemporary art there is more to a subterranean parallel between phenomenology and art than that.

Ours is a very self-conscious era, both with respect to philosophy and to artistic discovery. Today's artistic activity is often deliberately *deconstructive*. Its characteristics which virtually institutionalize shock, disjuncture, unfamiliarity, harbor also a series of deliberate tactics which are similar to those I have just used in deconstructing Necker Cubes.

One of John Cage's most talked about compositions features a stage setting with a piano. The player walks in, seats himself, acts as if he is about to play, remains stationary for an awkward length of time and then rises and exits. What has happened? Cage has, in effect, reversed a familiar figure/ground relationship. The framing of the composition and the silence of a composition—always elements of a musical performance—have here been enhanced. What is usually the foreground, dramatic presence, i.e., the music, is now absent and what was mere background, silence and the activity of the player, has become the present foreground.

Or, what does one do with a series of well-publicized photos of toilets by Edward Weston. The angles and contexts are such that the sensuous curves and shapes of these artifacts stand out, and of this activity the photographer says:

> I have been photographing our toilet, that glossy enameled receptacle of extraordinary beauty . . . here was every sensuous curve of the "human figure divine." . . . Never did the Greeks reach a more significant consummation to their culture.

A joke? Perhaps in part, but it is also an activity which isolates and resituates in such a way that sensuosity, curve and form are isolated from the usual familiar context.

Perception

In each of these cases the artist has been quite deliberately explicit about forcing the viewer or listener to take account of something disjunctive. In each of these cases something like a figure/ground reversal or the juxtaposition of familiar with unfamiliar context was employed as the means. The first result may be either shock, or the inability to see what is involved. Yet this first reaction is only that of a sedimented convention, the reaction of familiar ordinariness which has led us to believe that the cube only reverses itself with two variations.

Once seen in its new light, in its reversed or in its deconstructed possibilities, the artistic result may well reveal a deeper connection with something very ancient as well. For example, I recently underwent something of a conversion regarding an interpretation of Picasso's cubist period. I had always regarded cubism to be somewhat radical, a departure from many of the traditions of representationalist painting—and indeed it is, but only to a limited extent.

In technique, cubism breaks up surfaces and imposes various series of disjunctive planes in such a way that the object depicted may well border on unrecognizability. By historical accident, mostly familiar to our education in art, that is what we might suppose. We—in this case I—come upon the paintings themselves or their reproduced forms. The instance I have in mind is the series of distorted female portraits done by Picasso in his cubist phase. What stands out are the colors, planes and distortions which have faces looking at each other, etc., all familiar aspects of cubism. Only later, in a reversal of the order of Picasso's experienced history, did I come upon a biography of Picasso which included photos of his mistresses. And again later, I returned to the paintings. Suddenly, in a gestalt shock, I see each of them individually. I discover that Picasso's cubism has accurately caught essential features of the individual faces so that I can recognize each of the mistresses quite distinctly, one might even say, quite "representationally" in each cubist portrait. In short, while technically radical in some sense, these cubist portraits are also deeply traditional in that the painter has caught an essential feature of the reality he has experienced, the faces of his mistresses.

Phenomenologists claim that only through variations can the depth and richness of an entity be grasped. Artists have practiced, both explicitly and implicitly, this variational activity. But artists have one advantage—their practice is such that they have long learned the tricks of the trade: figure/ground reversals, juxtapositions of contexts, the isolation of dominant and recessive characteristics, the transformations of perspectives and the like. These deliberate uses of variations consitute the very core of practiced artistic method and are often quite self-consciously employed. In this sense the philosopher can indeed learn from the artist.

Contrarily, what the artist may learn from the philosopher, particularly the phenomenological philosopher, is that there is something like a *system* of perceptual possibilities which can be isolated, articulated and in effect applied. The logic of discovery which is made possible through an understanding of this open structure of perception poses a potential for a certain deliberateness which could well be incorporated into artistic activity. Phenomenological variations and artistic discovery in a deeper sense may turn out to be two sides of a single human activity.

Phenomenology is also necessarily quasi-artistic. Without the distancing possible through imaginative variations, the depth structures of phenomena would not likely reveal themselves. This is in no way to say the phenomenologist "creates" his phenomena in the way the artist does, but through the quasi-artistic process he employs, he discovers the structures of essential topographies. And if as philosopher he forever lacks the gracefulness of genuine artfulness, he also has the virtue of having systematically captured at least part of the essence of art for his own activity.

CHAPTER SIX
A Philosopher Listens

What does it mean to listen to music? For me this is a central question since I neither compose, perform, nor teach music—I belong to those limited to listening. But I am also a phenomenological philosopher, and although it would be inappropriate to introduce any technical "tribal language" here, I would point out that phenomenologists are supposed to pay careful, descriptive attention to experience. Moreover, we are supposed to note how the phenomenon in question appears and not try to go behind it or under it to offer an explanation. We "describe" rather than "explain." We hope in this way to point up important, and sometimes unnoticed, features of the phenomenon or at least to display the aspects of experience which are present prior to any theorizing about the experience.

In practice the phenomenologist often notes two things. First, the experience is almost always far richer, more complex and subtle, than one ordinarily takes it to be. Second, he finds that the language—and often the theory—about the phenomenon is cliché-ridden and bound by traditions and concepts which actually may hide important features of the experience. Thus he finds a problem in reformulating the description. His language seems to be inadequate to the discovered wealth of the experience and he finds himself expressing himself in metaphorical ways. Gradually, however, his struggles give birth to new expressions or give new meaning to old expressions. Through his descriptions the phenomenologist hopes to shed light upon both the particularities and the structures of human experience.

In this essay I will attempt to do this with listening. I shall begin by pointing up some of the most general features of auditory experience as they bear upon listening; then turn to a special problem which shows at least one way in which our traditions hide certain features of musical presence; and finally point to a suggestion about listening in musical experience.

I. General Features of Auditory Experience

(A) Sound and Sounds.

If we pay attention to our auditory experience, a simple set of distinctions suggests itself. Within experience there are multiple *sounds,* sound particulars. For example, within a brief period of taking note I find that I am conscious of the sound of my typewriter, of the faint voices from the TV in the other room, of the noises of traffic on the street, of the ticking of the clock, of the occasional bark of the dog. These multiple sounds all compete for my attention. But these are just bits of sound.

But we can attend not just to these particular features, but to the *field* of Sound, the whole, and note its characteristics. When I do this I discover that my auditory field is *never* empty. There is always Sound—even when I enter the anechoic chamber absolute silence is lacking. I hear my own blood rushing in my ears and the "hum" of my own nervous system. My field of Sound is never empty even if its concrete texture differs from time to time. The silences I experience are at best relative silences, actually contrasts rather than silences. Visitors from the city who visit my summer place in Vermont almost always remark about the silence of the country—until I point out the fullness of the sounds of the brook, the birds, the breeze, which, though not so blaring as the bedlam of the city, is full and constant. My field of Sound is constant in its sounding and in this sense the "music" of experience is always with us.

(B) Sounds and Attention.

The multiplicity of sounds competes for my attention. On one side I seem to have little control over their presence. Sounds intrude upon me. When they are harsh or sudden, my self-presence is disturbed to a high degree. The intrusive power of sound today has become a major psychological problem in our urban, technological, noisy culture. Our industrial Sound field is the almost constant presence of the whine of our engines.

But the control I do have is largely psychic. I can choose to attend, to attend in degree, or to diminish my attention within limits. This attention overrides many of the mere "physical" features of auditory presence. Thus, in spite of the fact that my typewriter is clacking noisily, I can note, "Is that strange, barely perceived whistle in the motor of my furnace a sign that it needs oil?" Or, if listening to music, I can make the faint strains of the flute "stand out" even against the dominance of the trombone.

Not only may I attend to one sound—make it "stand out" in the center of my attention—to the near exclusion or at least relative exclusion of other sounds, but I may concentrate upon particular features of a sound to the relative exclusion of others. Thus the sound of the bird sounds like a musical note with a particular melody. And *for me* the melodic quality of the song is what "stands out." But note here, by way of anticipation of the next section, that what is important for me may not be at all important for the bird. It may be that the signal he is conveying to his peers is actually to be found not in the melodic quality of his "song" but in the barely discerned "clicks" which are included within the total presence of his sounding. In this case, my traditional metaphor of bird's sounding as "song" may keep me from noting what, to his mind, is precisely the important feature. My "control" over sound is my attention and its selectivity. But this very selectivity is both what "reveals" something about sounds to me and at the same time "conceals" other aspects of sound.

(C) The "Space" of Sound.

In the main there are two "spatial" aspects to sound. Sounds may come from a direction—they are localizable to an amazingly precise degree. We know where the sound comes from so that in some cases the sound-appearance surprises us as in the case of the jet plane whose sound trails its visual appearance so badly. And in ordinary experience the localization of sounds play an extremely important role.

But at the same time the sounds are localizable, they also display themselves as a surrounding. It is this dimension of sound which tends to be utilized in music. We find ourselves "immersed" in sound and our best built stereos and auditoria seek to emphasize this effect. Our heads are "filled with sound" to such a degree that in the maximal case even the usual inner-outer distinctions are blurred.

The encompassing characteristic of Sound space is the second feature which lends itself to the seductivity of music. Sound commands and Sound surrounds us. In this sense music is not only present, but omnipresent and my only flight is my ability to retire psychically. Music, like God, encompasses us and at least attempts to overwhelm us. Thus music, like the gods, can be either demonic or salvific.

(D) Music as "Language" or Language as "Music."

It has often been noted that music and language are closely related. Both, in their living forms, are creatures of auditory experience. And both may be "reduced" to writing—not without effect. First, let us note some of the experiential bases for the analogy between music and language.

Perhaps the simplest and shortest way to illustrate the analogy is by looking at a few examples of parallelisms between music and language. In our "mother tongue," we take the words, the grammar, and even the flow of the conversation for granted. It is so familiar that we don't think twice about things. But note that in a given conversation we have subtle expectations. Although we may not be able to predict exactly, given a context, what the next speaker will say, we do know roughly what to expect.

The same may be said of music. Perhaps the best example known to me is that form of relatively informal "conversation" among accomplished jazz musicians. They intuitively know what progressions "fit" the "language" and which do not. Each "statement" is in the same "language" just as our conversations remain within a context. By contrast, note what playing a piece which has been either strictly memorized or which is played from a score does. Here the "language" has been canned—it is like a classic drama in which each speech has already been foreordained. Expectation here follows different cues, is less intuitive, Again, before passing to the next section, I would note that in either case the language of the music has its own logic which must be understood by the player—and by the listener if he or she is to follow the train of thought.

A second set of examples which establishes a parallelism between music and language may be noted in the process of learning a new language. When I hear a new tongue for the first time I may not even be sure the speaker is speaking a language at all. His tongue appears to me a babble which has no apparent meaning although I may very generally suspect it is a language. Only after much listening do patterns begin to appear which appear to be related in turn to possible meanings. In fact, I may not know what to look for at first. For example, for me it was relatively easy to learn to understand German because the Germans do roughly the same thing with words that we do. I could recognize individual words and the music of German was similar to the familiar English. But the first contacts with spoken French were utterly incomprehensible to me in spite of the fact that in the written form it is much closer to English in both spelling and meaning. The way the words ran together, glided into one another so that I couldn't even tell where one began and the other ended, plus the use of quite different accents and intonations at first posed a rather thorough confusion.

In a similar way, when I first heard Indian music, it seemed doubtful that it was music at all—I didn't know what to look for. The constant whine of the sympathetic strings on the sitar and the minute unaccustomed changes, let alone the less distinct separation of notes, left me in a state of not knowing the language. (Note that Indian music divides not only into the tones of our scale, but employs twenty-two intervals of semi-tones, micro-tones, etc., within the octave. Furthermore, notes are not divided neatly but are deliberately "glided" into one another.) Its musical language was at first mere babble or noise. And just as I must employ intense concentration to learn a language, so I also had to concentrate to learn to appreciate Indian musical language.

And, once learned, a new language reveals a new world. Whether language reflects the world of the speaker or actually forms it, is not here the primary issue. What is at issue is that, once formed, the world of the speaker of English and of the speaker of Chinese is different. It has always seemed a shame to me to reduce humanities requirements in languages precisely because to be human calls for a recognition of the human in many perspectives and I know of no better way to do this than through languages.

Music is a language and music speaks—many tongues. "Our" music, i.e., Western music with its keyboard is but one family of languages which today is being changed in the introduction of new scales, instruments, and notations.

II. Music and Notation

If music is like language in its auditory appearance, it is like language in a second way as well. Some languages have been reduced to writing and some have not and we are well aware today that there are large differences between literate and nonliterate cultures. The differences are not between *completeness* or *complexity;* as linguists are quick to point out, all languages are complex and complete in relation to their cultural forms.

But a culture which has a written language is able to *accumulate* knowledge in its records—it makes its words come "to stand" in a preserved written word. But this advantage which reveals things to us about the past, about what happened, about many things, also conceals. Writing "reduces" a living tongue and a "reduction" is a simplification. Thus writing leaves out gestures, tones of voice, the peculiarities of the speaker's style, nuances and innuendos which can be noted only in the spoken word. In short, a reduction to written language preserves only an essential, but bare conceptuality. Indeed, our sense of "objectivity" is very closely related to the reduction of live speech into an "object" which is the evidence of the written word. (Obviously, also, we are on the verge of a very new reduction in today's records, now no longer merely written, but preserved, made to stand in tapes, videotapes, and phonograph records.)

This same reduction occurred with music. The introduction of a notation reduced musical forms into noted ones. But just as writing affects a culture, so does notation effect a musical language. One early and formative effect was clearly due to the Greeks who approached their music theoretically and mathematically. "Good sounds" were those which represented certain ideal forms, basically harmonic. Our musical grammar has been basically harmonic and, I suspect, tends to continue to be so in much of music education. It also directed what sounds were permissible to a certain extent. (Our notation would be incapable of dealing with a twenty-two tone scale, thus we exclude certain sounds from our musical language. We "conceal" a part of Sound.)

Secondly, our attitude has been highly influenced by our theorizing. We compose, put together, our music. In certain periods some theoretical constructions were considered more valuable than others—these rules rather than those ought to be followed. But apart from our folk traditions—which incidentally often were associated with the nonliterate part of society—we did not question the basic theoretical concern with music. Musicology is the metaphysics of music education.

I am not trying to be derogatory of this concern; to the contrary, it is our theoretical attitude which has made the West so uniquely successful in the world. But I am trying to point out that our attitude is also a concealment of other possibilities. It is far from obvious that our musical language is superior to other musical languages. I have already noted that all living languages are complex and the same applies to music in some degree. If one compares the sitar with the piano, for example, it does not seem to me at all obvious that one is more complex than the other. Eighty-eight keys are perhaps more than seven playing strings with twenty sympathetic strings—but there are also nineteen or twenty frets on the sitar. Moreover, the sitar player plays with infinite possibilities of tension on his strings to get the micro-tones which are possible. Difference, not complexity, is what is important. The subtle, whining, gliding, transposed and reverberated notes of the sitar speak a far different language than the sparkling "atoms" of notes, clearly distinguishable and delineated on our piano. The Western emphasis on the rational, clear, and distinct contrasts with the Eastern on continuities and unities. The musical language just as the spoken language reveals a different world. And there are as many worlds as there are languages.

III. Listening

Music is neither its notation nor its theory. And sound is not its qualities nor its measurements. This, in spite of the obvious importance of theory and measurement for our metaphysics. The point is this: there is a sense in which the naïve listener retains an advantage over his learned peers. He, like the child who only up to a certain age may learn easily and naturally a number of languages, may, by listening, learn of the wider possibilities of musical languages. To listen is to let the music speak on its own ground.

But the problem is that none of us are any longer naïve listeners. We are already plunged into the thought formed by our mother tongues. Only by a "second naïveté" can we approach a purity of listening. This second naïveté comes only by concentration and a willingness to suspend our own tongues and beliefs.

Heidegger holds that the only way to get to the essential in things, in this case, music, is by "letting them be" or by letting them "show themselves." He means that our naïveté ought to consist not so much in looking for particular things, but in excluding as much as possible our performed notions concerning things. We let things speak for themselves.

What I have been saying about music and language relates to this as well. We used to teach languages in a backward way, a way which all too well emphasized our theoretical "metaphysics."

We began by first painfully teaching grammar and theory and then "applying" it to a living language. Clearly, this was not the way children learned, nor was it very effective. Today we have—rightly, I believe—begun to reinvert the emphasis through our use of total immersion and other techniques which begin by using, by speaking, language. Living language precedes grammar just as music precedes musicology. We *begin* by listening (and playing), by allowing ourselves to be immersed in the sounds, to be commanded by them, to allow them to flow over us and into us no matter how strange they might seem.

Music will speak but it will speak in many tongues and those tongues will be rich and give forth strange new sounds as well as familiar old ones. To me, the best music education is one which emphasizes the multilingual. As a "naïve" listener I will harken to all the voices.

CHAPTER SEVEN
Intercultural Perception

I. Introduction

Towards the end of his career, Merleau-Ponty, that most astute philosopher of perception, concluded that perception itself was guided by culture:

> What I maintain is that: there is an informing of perception by culture which enables us to say that culture is perceived—there is a dilatation of perception, a carrying over of the *Aha Erlebnis* of "natural" perception to instrumental relations . . . which obliges us to put in continuity the perceptual openness to the world and the openness to the cultural world.[1]

He used as an example what many would assume to be a basic and primitive perception, the Euclidian perception of depth in paintings:

> I say that the Renaissance perspective is a cultural fact, that perception itself is polymorphic and that if it becomes Euclidian this is because it allows itself to be oriented by the system.[2]

Such claims by a philosopher, particularly one known for his stance that perception is primary, hold a significant set of implications for the problems of intercultural communication.

If it is true that culture informs perception, not just at the macrocosmic level nor at those levels of perception where multiple interpretation is obvious, but at the most primitive levels of such phenomena as spatial perception, then the polymorphy of perception is one of the most enigmatic problems which may be embedded in the task of communication.

I shall address this problem, the problem of polymorphic perception, by developing a set of examples of both macro and microcosmic perceptions of spatiality and relate these to a model for understanding polymorphic perception from a phenomenological perspective. The intertwining of even primitive perception and culture will be shown, and while I shall not address the applications of this model to practical communication problems, my claim will be that the problem of cultural perception will have been outlined more fully.

II. Macro and Microcosmic Perceptions of Spatiality

Perception is deeply involved in our most primitive actions of which locomotion or movement in space may be taken as a primary case. A geometrizing or abstract analysis of human locomotion, of the type most likely to occur in psychology, is itself an instance of a certain understanding of bodily activity. Phenomenologists have frequently pointed out that such an approach to our orientation in space is both reductive and self-verifying. That is, the standard empirical psychologies in setting up experimental controls not only remove the result from the life situation, but this removal itself is what creates the condition of the possibility of the usual conclusions drawn.

Such a geometrized or abstract conclusion is intended to be culture-free, but by the very virtue with which such a claim could be made it is also human activity-free. Living humans embedded in cultures simply are unrecognizable from the electronicslike descriptions of psychology textbooks. Such a method would not reveal to us the primitivity of a culturally informed perception like the perception of Euclidian space in a Renaissance perspective painting.

Yet the very perception of human spatiality may be shown to

be culturally informed. A simple autobiographical example may suffice. A number of years ago while working at MIT one of my colleagues was a rabbi from eastern Europe. We frequently had occasion to enter into serious discussions and debate. I always felt extremely uncomfortable in those discussions and it took me a rather long time to figure out why.

At first I thought maybe it was our age difference, or maybe some mode of expression, because I always felt on the defensive, as if I were being pushed into a stance I didn't want to take. Eventually, however, I discovered what it was. Whenever one of these intense discussions occurred he would stand very close to me and literally place his face within a foot or eighteen inches of mine. In response I would back away until I was a more comfortable two to three feet from him. I was experiencing a difference in the way two cultural and ethnic groups make conversation, an experience of bodily spatiality in a conversational world. I wordlessly experienced, that is perceived, his bodily stance as threatening, aggressive, demanding. I later discovered when I talked about this with him that contrarily he experienced my retreat as coolness, reticence and perhaps a refusal to communicate.

We both had very different perceptual-cultural senses of the appropriate bodily orientation in conversational space. Our very distances to the other were variant and such variations are concretely felt. Here at a relatively micro-level is an instance of culturally informed perception. Such culturally informed perception, regardless of our mutual intentions, in its difference caused the problem of misperceived communication.

Conversational space and the bodily spatiality which it entails is a near-space experience with numerous implications. At a more macro-level the same culturally informed perceptions may be found. In this case my example will point out profound variants in the way we experience spatial motion. The example comes from European perceptions of navigational motion contrasted with those of the Micronesians.

When Westerners travel in ships or boats it is usual, perhaps nearly universal, to experience the boat as going somewhere. That is, it is the boat which is moving and the sea or earth remains stable. Contrarily, in a certain type of Micronesian navigation the sailor experiences the sea as in motion with the boat as the stable point of reference. At a sensory level both such cultural perceptions are possible. One can look down at a bow wave, see the sea slipping by the hull of the boat, and within the context it could be that the sea is moving by, or that the boat is moving through the waves. (The same phenomenon could be observed were the boat to be in a high current river. Here the bow wave could be perceived as a high speed up river while the boat with respect to the shore remains stationary.) In short, we have a species of relativity gestalt here which gains its ultimate sense from an implied point of view. This in turn relates to two quite different concepts of navigation.

European navigation conceives of the earth as a grid and the ship's position as a location upon the grid—it secretly favors a bird's eye view of motion with the fixed bird's eye as the stationary point. In the Micronesian example one might say that the navigator's body is the fixed point and that all motion occurs with respect to that experienced point. This is a cultural perceptual gestalt switch. What is needed is a deeper understanding of the topography of perception itself.

III. A Model for Polymorphic Perception

That there can even be such a thing as cultural variation within perception implies something about perception itself. As Merleau-Ponty noted, "perception itself is polymorphic . . . and allows itself to be oriented."[3] But does this polymorphy itself have a shape? I contend that it does and that the shape of polymorphy is one of multi-stability.[4] Visual examples of multi-stability, such as the Necker Cube (see the more extensive working out of this example in Chapter Five), can be worked out phenomenologically to show that there is an indefinite, if not infinite, field of possibilities nevertheless structured in such ambiguous drawings. Necker Cubes, for instance, are not bi-stable drawings, but have at least

Intercultural Perception

---

two three-dimensional reversals, and at least one two-dimensional possibility, etc. But in each case each variation is mutually exclusive and distinct. Its "ambiguity" is not fuzzy, but serieslike in extension. And in this case one might argue for a horizontally shaped structure of multi-stability. Each visual possibility is "equal" and artibrary, although relative to an interpretative context.

I return briefly to the Necker Cube example from chapter five for a different purpose here.

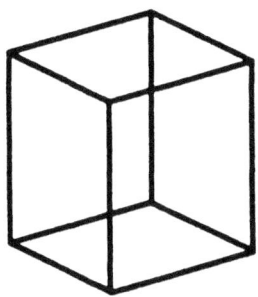

Once we have established that the cube has more than bi-stability, and once we have become familiar with how to see it as forward-facing cube (3-d^f), rearward-facing cube (3-d^r), the "flat" (2-d) and subsequent three-dimensional variants, we may be said to have ascended from literal to possible levels. Phenomenologically, this is a gain, an ascent from the merely empirical to the essential or possible. It is a gain in perspective which itself is irreversible in that once seen, the viewer never again can be simply naïve, at least with respect to the actually so-experienced multi-stability.

There is a parallel to this movement within the social sciences, particularly anthropology. Cultural possibilities are the anthropologist's field upon which a topography may be developed. There is also a danger here. The ascent from simple cultural chauvinism or parochialism is a genuine ascent and the so-called "relativism" of such a perspective is to my mind a necessary first step. The danger, however, is to remain to play amidst the relativities, however genuine they may be.

Anthropology to date has not developed too many topographies. I suspect with respect to kinship patterns and the incest taboo it has. But with respect to much of human variant activity we still remain ourselves collectors. I am not blaming the discipline for this state of affairs because it is the phenomenon itself which is so complex—the state of the art is not yet at the particle physics stage because in part the phenomenon itself is more complex even than an atom.

I am suggesting that in spite of complexity, a multi-stability model of cultural perception is helpful. Cultures and their perception contexts function like stabilities.

Each of the variations is relatively stable, relatively autonomous and each is an alternative to the other or temporally exclusive in its moment of appearance. And each has its hermeneutic device or "cultural myth" which informs the perception. Here we have a parallel to the situation which exemplifies human cultures. Perceptions occur in a world and are relative to the stance and context taken. Contrarily, there is no perception without this variability. From this we should suspect that there is equivalently no supracultural stance possible. Perceptions are always perceptions from somewhere. Perceptions imply embodiment and embodiment a position.

IV. Cross-cultural Communication

If it is the case that each distinct appearance of a culturally informed microview of a Necker Cube implies both a cultural embeddedness and some form of position from which the sight is taken, and if this model reveals the lack of a supracultural position from which to judge cultural perceptions, it remains the case that something has been significantly gained through the variations.

If an initial viewer remained satisfied with the singular veracity of his own version of the cube, we could now from the perspective of multiple variations declare him naïve. It is not that his version is wrong, far from it, since his version is repeatable and never disappears from possibility. Rather, it is that taken by itself it is inadequate to discern the range of possibilities.

This insight, however, is not attained through a supracultural position. It is attained through variations which instantiate each appearance successively. It is a polymorphic position which retains the necessity of an embodied position.

That there is a positive analogy here for the problems of intercultural communication should be obvious. There are biculturally able individuals. The Lawrence of Arabia person who enters two cultures thoroughly is better able to inform each of the location of the differences. But one must also be wary of stretching the analogy too far.

The "minicultures" of the visual experiment are shallow "cultures." The reasons for this should be obvious enough. Cube viewing is a phenomenon which is relatively shallow—it entails very little to change our views on its possibilities and it commits us to only the most superficial changes in perspective. This is not the case with intercultural differences.

Our cultural entailment always involves a deep and relatively long history, for example, in the form of living languages which take time and learning to enter. Insofar as each language is itself part of that which culturally informs, it entails this deep and long personal and social history. And a language itself belongs to yet a longer and deeper cultural history. All of this is the horizon within which perception is informed.

Perception, however, remains basic. It involves the very way we orient ourselves in our environment and implicates the very gestures we make. The macho way a South American gaucho strides implies a whole attitude towards others, women and the world. The way my rabbi friend converses entails a whole way in which relations to others takes shape. Not to have learned both the verbal and nonverbal languages of such actions leaves one always at the level of the abstract and open to the grossest misunderstandings.

Am I saying that cross-cultural communication is impossible? No, but it is difficult in the extreme, and it is open to severe miscommunication without awareness of the perceptual nuances which inevitably occur. The political confusions of the world are massive evidence of this lack of multicultural ability. How are we to understand the haggling which goes on concerning the Iranians unless we see the world the way they do? How are we to understand the situation regarding the "Gang of Four" unless we understand the special language of insult in a shame as contrasted to a guilt culture?

If cross-cultural communication is difficult because it entails our deepest and longest held beliefs and perceptions about the world, at least what the paradigm of culturally informed perceptions shows is that the most basic question is one about how the world is seen. That, it seems to me, is the primary contribution phenomenology can make to the problems of cross-cultural communication. The first question is one of how does one perceive the world.

Contrary to those who would claim some base which is simply precultural or culture-free, my examples tend to shed doubt upon the neutrality of any perception. Perception in its very structure is open textured and polymorphic, in part because the world itself is complex and open. If that makes the task difficult by virtue of the fact that the world is open to multiple interpretations and by virtue of the fact that our perception is polymorphic, at least the polymorphy itself has a shape. The relative autonomies of multi-stabilities, I suggest, are the ways in which we may begin to appreciate and understand the problems of cross-culturally differing perceptions. When we become adept at polymorphic viewing we will have made the first steps towards genuine cross-cultural understanding.

PART THREE
Interpretation

CHAPTER EIGHT
Phenomenology and the Later Heidegger

I. Introduction

In scholarly circles there remain many enigmas concerning the relationship between Edmund Husserl and Martin Heidegger, both in respect to their personal relations and in respect to their philosophical influence upon each other. Perhaps most obviously one may note the profound respect paid Husserl by Heidegger in some of the early works, most notably *Being and Time* where Heidegger acknowledges that *only* through phenomenology is fundamental ontology possible.[1] Conversely, there is at least indirect evidence that Heidegger exerted an influence upon Husserl, particularly in the *Crisis* where, on almost every page, there are Heidegger-like terms and phrases and there is a thematic turn which approximates much of *Being and Time*.

But in Heidegger's own work, both from the outset and then later, there is a gradual dropping of explicit terminological usage relating to phenomenology which has led a number of noted scholars to contend that either Heidegger abandoned phenomenology or so modified it that it could no longer be recognized as phenomenology. Herbert Spiegelberg's thesis which, in part, revolves around the lack of specific terms and methodological steps in Heidegger, comes closest to claiming that Heidegger (has) abandoned phenomenology. More prevalent is the thesis of the "turn" in which there is presumed to be some dramatic change between the "early" Heidegger (I) and the "later" Heidegger (II, if Richardson or II and III if Versenyi). In this case the analysis of *Dasein* which was recognizably phenomenological, gives way to *Seinsfragen* which are no longer recognizable as phenomenology.

An even more general opinion is that while the "early" Heidegger remains generally within the philosophical and even phenomenological traditions, the "later" Heidegger has become so obscure that it remains doubtful whether or not he ought to be displaced to a more "literary" category. Apart from revealing the deeply held Positivist prejudices which still permeate the philosophical world, this judgment revolves around what I believe to be a deeply held misunderstanding concerning Heidegger.

The reading of Heidegger which I wish to defend here is one which retains for him a deep connection with the central insights of phenomenology and which may be stated in terms of a series of gradually narrowed theses: (1) In the most general terms I am defending a *unitary* development in relation to Heidegger's thought-paths, but in addition, this unity remains within the spirit if not the letter of phenomenology. At the center of this development is the adaptation of an essentially *descriptive*—as contrasted with an argumentative, explanatory, or metaphysically speculative—"method." I regard the clarification and development of a radically descriptive-interpretative (hermeneutic) method to be a core factor in any phenomenology and am claiming that this factor shows itself in the "later" Heidegger.

(2) At the same time I must obviously admit that within the Heideggerian development of phenomenology there is an *adaptation* of phenomenology to his own questions and direction of inquiry. But this adaptation is not something which occurs later, it occurs from the outset. *Being and Time* already sees in phenomenology a questioning backwards which is simultaneously a questioning outwards towards the limits of phenomenology. Heidegger terms this the hermeneutic dimension of phenomenology. "The phenomenology of Dasein is a *hermeneutic* in the primordial signification of the word. . . ."[2] Description, in other words, for Heidegger is less guided by the mathematicological heuristic model of Husserl than by the traditions of interpreta-

tion, by an implicitly historico-temporal paradigm.

Yet, in spite of the paradigm shift which occurs at the very beginning of Heidegger's explicit use of phenomenology, the core signification of a descriptive approach to phenomena remains constant. No hypothetical, no deduced, no inferred entities, no constructed posits are to be given primacy in the ontological schematism whatever it turns out to be like. Rather, the spirit of description is such that *"die Sache selbst"* must show themselves. If in Heidegger that showing is a *shining* phenomenon in contrast to the more mundane examples of Husserl, it is nevertheless in keeping with the descriptive spirit.

(3) However, to narrow the interpretation of phenomenology in the later Heidegger, I shall select one pervasive theme of inquiry in the later Heidegger, the enigma of the *horizon*. My contention is that it is in the presencing of what may be called *horizons-phenomena* that most of the crucial issues for a phenomenological philosophy arise and that it is here that the later Heidegger finds his most acute struggle with fundamental thought. The problem of the horizon is, of course, not the only problem which the later Heidegger addresses. It is the problem, however, which may be most easily developed to show the way in which phenomenology occurs in the recent thought of Heidegger. Furthermore, the problem of the horizon shows the direction of the *radicalization* of phenomenology which Heidegger develops. But far from breaking with phenomenology, some of the enigmatic notions of the later Heidegger show their essential continuity with a *radically* descriptive method. It is, once again, *die Sache selbst* which calls for, which demands precisely, the semingly strange linguistic usage which Heidegger employs for description.

Thus, if I may summarize my theses in the most outrageous way I can, I would say that: The later Heidegger is doing a radical phenomenological description of horizons-phenomena and that it is the showing forth of that phenomenon itself which demands the radical language which emerges in Heidegger's thought. Moreover, there is a sense in which, if language is ever "literal," this description is literal and not metaphorical language when it is understood within the context of a descriptive phenomenological development. (From a Heideggerian point of view metaphor belongs to metaphysics.)

II. Husserl and Heidegger

To defend these theses I contend that there is an inherent demand that the defense itself be essentially phenomenological. Thus from the outset my problem is not that of proof-texting, but of explicating a set of phenomena and their relation to the methodological procedures called phenomenology. The hermeneutic circle in which one must know in order to understand, but understand in order to know, has its place in phenomenology as we all know—but there is a certain asymmetry to where the circle "begins." In the Husserlian sense it is quite clear that the first move is one which hopes to open up and clear the experiential field as the first order of business. Thus there is a sense in which the circle "begins" with the "knowing" which leads to understanding, or, there is a sense in which the "seeing" reveals the "saying" or what can be said. This, I take it, is essential in the first return to *die Sache selbst*.

I am not, of course, claiming that this "beginning" is also the end, merely that it is the beginning. And in relation to phenomenology in the later Heidegger, this is also the beginning which I wish to make in relation to the position which I wish to defend. Thus, if I am radically phenomenological, I must find a way to let the phenomenon "show itself" in the hopes that the phenomenon will "teach" its own lessons which in this case is the appropriateness of the radical descriptions Heidegger employs.

My approach in this context is to follow Heidegger, not by way of the usual textual analysis, but by way of developing examples, in the main examples which Heidegger has himself inaugurated in his discussion. In this I am merely following the example set by Husserl not as a writer but *as teacher*, an example which apparently was taken seriously by Heidegger. To try to understand Husserlian phenomenology merely by reading the usually programmatic texts—a task taken up by too many interpreters already—is often to miss learning what is going on.

In his fascinating contribution to the Niemeyer *Festgabe* describing his own way into phenomenology, Heidegger not only confesses a certain inability to comprehend phenomenology which he had known through texts for years prior to learning under the *teaching* of Husserl, but indicates that the teaching was always *first* a matter of learning to experience or to "see." "Husserl's teaching took place in the form of a step-by-step training in phenomenological 'seeing' which at the same time demanded that one relinquish the untested use of philosophical knowledge. But it also demanded that one give up introducing the authority of the great thinkers into the conversation."[3] Heidegger goes on to say that he himself practices such phenomenological "seeing," teaching and learning and that it was through this that his own radical reclamation and reinterpretation of the Greeks came about. It was the phenomena which taught the lesson—what was "seen" allowed what was now a radical, new understanding to take its place in fundamental thinking.

I believe that Heidegger, the so-called later Heidegger, continues to follow precisely that direction. He calls upon us to "see" in a certain way and once we attain that "seeing" then what he says not only ceases to be odd, it must be understood as radically and descriptively appropriate.

Moreover, Heidegger himself provides the example, the paradigm, which shows the way into the horizon-phenomenon with which he deals. The example is in one sense an extremely simple one, yet its careful and fastidious examination reveals precisely what Heidegger is after. The example I have in mind is the one offered in *Gelassenheit* which as a text already has the structure of a teaching situation. The dialogue, rather than the methodological, scholarly treatise, is the occasion for the introduction of what seems on the surface an impenetrable maze of language.

The example which animates and illustrates the bulk of Heidegger's talk of Region (*Gegend*), is that of the *visual field*. It is by developing in a paradigmatic fashion the various aspects and dimensions which may be noted phenomenologically in the visual field that I hope to show the implicit phenomenology of Heidegger. The advantage of this strategy, of taking a single example to stand for the entire range of horizons-phenomena, lies in the simplicity of finding the relevant aspects within experience.

However, before plunging directly into the example, it may be advisable to set up a certain minimal set of functional equivalents between the Husserlian and the Heideggerian interpretations of phenomenology including minimal remarks about the divergences which also obtain. At the heart of the functional similarity lies a notion which I call simply a method of *correlations-apriori*. This method arises as the result of the phenomenological discovery and development of *intentionality*. It remains a core feature of phenomenological description whether interpreted "transcendentally" or "existentially."

With Husserl the *correlation-apriori* takes several forms, but that of the *Cartesian Meditations* serves as well as any to illustrate the correlation. The intentional relation is there displayed as:

Ego-cogito-cogitatum.

Intentionally, that which is "thought," the experienc*ed* is the *cogitatum* (noema), while the act of thought or thinking activity is the *cogito* (noesis). The "ego," in strictest terms, is the indirectly arrived at "thinking" pole of the correlation. Within the limits of the phenomenological *epoché* the correlation is strictly maintained: no "object" except in relation or correlation with its mode of givenness, no "subject" except in relation to that which is intended, a "world."

Moreover, not only is the correlation strictly maintained, but there is a movement or order which the description which takes place within the correlation must follow. What appears "first" is the terminus of the intentional relation, the cogitatum (noema). Only reflexively is the nature of the act of "knowing" and its organizing center (ego) known. The route to the "subject" is indirect in the sense that it is read from the "object" and in terms of a strict correlation with the "object." This *correlation-apriori* which defines the phenomenological method is the radical alternative to "cartesianism" for Husserl.

Functionally, the same model of a *correlation-apriori*, though in a differently interpreted form, may be found for Heidegger. As Merleau-Ponty has already noted, "Heidegger's 'being-in-the-world' appears only against the background of the phenomenological reduction."[4] But in Heidegger's use of it, the basically epistemological focus is transformed into an existential ontology. The correlation is now phrased as:

In-der Welt-Sein.

Note, now, three facts of the Heideggerian form of the correlation as a mode of "being-in": (a) first, it is the World which apears "first" and the first reflections are upon the World and its Worldhood. This parallels the order of the original correlation, only now the concept is both widened and existentialized. (b) Second, being-in likewise replaces the essentially epistemological cogito activity with that of being-found-in (*Befindlichkeit*), a state of being. (c) Finally, note that the formulation now does one more thing, it leaves the bearer of the activity entirely implicit—who as being in the world is, of course, *Dasein,* but Dasein is not placed directly in the equation. This is at one and the same time Heidegger's refusal to enter the subjectivistic trap opened for Husserl in modeling his correlation even heuristically upon a Cartesian paradigm. What could already be noted in relation to the reflexive knowing of the "subject" in the Husserlian context is here radicalized so that the "subject"—now become Dasein—is always implicit. To make Dasein "transparent in its being" calls for the full analysis of Worldhood by which Dasein's situation, its *being-here* (Dasein) in a nice Heideggerian descriptive literalism, is revealed.

However, the only point I wish to draw attention to here is the essential *functional* parallelism of the ego-cogito-cogitatum with that of being-in-the-world. Although radically different in interpretation, "methodologically" they function in the same manner. What is "first" is the appearance, the phenomenon. and from it, the reflexive clarification of the knower or the exister is gradually clarified. It is from this base that we may turn to the selected model for horizons-phenomena from which I may explicate my thesis concerning phenomenology in the later Heidegger.

III. Phenomenological Exposition

The first step in the explication lies in the careful display of the paradigm sanctioned by Heidegger. And although the choice of a single example, the visual field, and a single text, *Gelassenheit*, is in a sense a narrow focus, the intensity of the focus allows the phenomenon to be more clearly illuminated. In *Gelassenheit* the dialogue between the teacher, the scholar and the scientist opens with what appears as an ongoing discussion of the question of man, of knowledge as representation, and of the question of will. It seems to be the case that the teacher is trying to lead his listeners into what is at first a strange path, a thinking which is a radically different and non-representational thinking. To explicate the meaning of this path the teacher allows the example of the visual field to emerge as the paradigm. I think it not accidental or inappropriate that Heidegger allows the scientist to identify the phenomenon as the visual field: "You describe, once again, the horizon which encircles the view of a thing—the field of vision." (Der Horizont, den Sie da noch einmal beschreiben, ist der Gesichtskreis, der die Aussicht umkreist.)[5] The visual field as the example, now needs to be preliminarily noted.

To further simplify matters, I shall diagram the illustration, using descriptive language to characterize the various aspects of the phenomenon. The visual field is first the totality of, or expanse of, what is visually present "before me." It may be thought of as the visual "opening" to the world. It lies before me and within it there come into being whatever visual presences I may discern. Thus I may look out my study window and see a panorama of forest and mountains in southern Vermont. But the field is also structured variably. I may notice in particular the top of Mt. Bromley and when I do so I may say both that Mt. Bromley "stands out" within the expanse of the visual field and that I "focus upon" Mt. Bromley (noema and noesis are correlated). But this situation also displays a feature of visual experience if I specify it further. I note that what is the focal-core, Mt. Bromley, attains its greatest specificity when *fixed* near or at the center of my visual field (a).

Secondly, reflectively I may realize that this central or focal

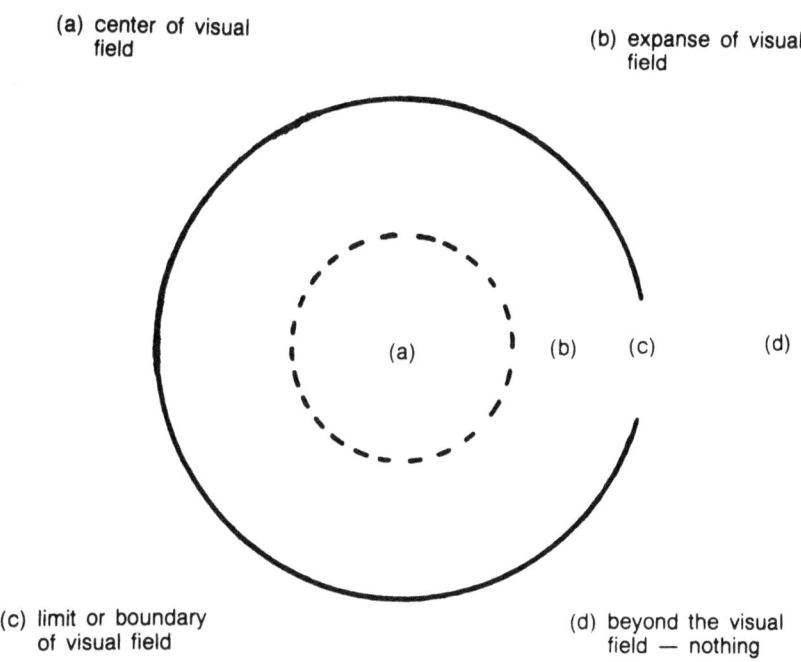

(a) center of visual field
(b) expanse of visual field
(c) limit or boundary of visual field
(d) beyond the visual field — nothing

clarity is not present alone or isolated from the expanse of the field (b), but always stands in a relationship to a being-situated-within that expanse (b). Thirdly, if I now begin to take account of the field, I eventually note that there is a vague, very implicit, and sometimes even unnoticed *limit* or *boundary* to the visual field (c), beyond which I may be said to see *nothing* (d).

If now I return to this noting of the visual field in a Husserlian mode, I could redescribe each feature in terms of a stricter noematic-noetic analysis. I would describe minutely the features of the various core appearances and how they are explicitly clear when compared to the degrees of implicitness which the surrounding and situating field phenomena show. I could also elaborate upon the greater vagueness of the extreme fringe or periphery of the field, etc. Then I could return and noetically describe the various acts which "constitute" the appearances as correlations with those appearances. I would then speak of the act of focusing, the act of taking in a panaramic vista, the act of indirectly enticing the horizon as limit, etc. I would also have to describe the various "internal" relations which obtain within the field presence. I would note that there never is a thing-in-itself except as situated and ordered contextually by that which surrounds it, and thereby I would note the *ratio* or thing to field, etc.

But the primary problem lies further along the way. It lies in identifying two dimensions of horizons-phenomena. The first dimension occurs in relation to *things*. Each thing within the visual field presents itself with the signification: "transcendent." This is in the sense that the thing is present as always concealing something of itself from me, but in such a way that the sense of concealment is always *in relation to* what is present. Here the Husserlian notion of *Abschatuungen* emerges. Profiles are presented, but always with the significance that there is latent and implicit another profile (and an interior, etc.) which is *not* present. There is in the "showing" of each thing a co-meant "withdrawing" which is a horizontal dimension.

The second dimension of a horizon-phenomenon, however, is more easily overlooked. It is locatable in relation to the *entirety* of the visual field and is first identified with the limit or extreme periphery of the field as a whole, (c). The field, as an intentional phenomenon, is *my* "opening" to the world, but the world also "transcends" this finitude of perspective although it is not given except within this finitude of perspective. The "opening" as the field displays itself as having a border, a limit, a *horizon* in the strong sense. Granted that the horizon is not clear and distinct—it withdraws and escapes explicit noting—yet I can glimpse its escaping moment. But it also displays some similarities to the particular horizon of a thing. First, the significance of the "transcendence" of the world is given *in relation to* what is strictly present. The expanse which "exceeds" my "opening" also "transcends" what is present, but is noted only in relation to that presence.

Second, the horizon in the strong sense also *situates* the visual field as a whole, but in what at first seems an odd sense. What is given inside or within the field is situated by, surrounded by, *Nothing,* (d). This Nothing, however, has a stronger sense than mere absence, but preliminarily we may speak of the field itself as bounded by Nothing.

Here, of course, the Heideggerian thesis has already appeared. My beginning use of Heidegger-like descriptions is purposeful, but what I wish to call attention to is that the descriptions, even if unusual, are *not* metaphorical, but descriptive in a much stricter sense. What is unusual is, in fact, not the description, but the phenomenon. The horizon is that which escapes note, is farthest from our attention, is the most latent and implicit within experience and thus it is to be expected that the language for such phenomena would also be "unusual" in relation to central ordinariness. To describe the limit, the border, the beyondness of *Nothing* as that which is *nonpresent* emerges as the enigma of the horizon.

Only after this display and extension of the Heideggerian example is it possible to turn to the *Gelassenheit* text to show how this enigma remains within the realm of descriptive analysis. What is at stake is a choice between moving back into a metaphysical, argumentative, hypothetical context and remaining descriptive at the limits. Whatever "Nothing" is for description, it cannot be posited speculatively (I am well aware that this sentence is *not* properly Heideggerian!).

If now I continue the exposition by pairing the Husserlian rubric with the "later" Heidegger of *Gelassenheit* I may be able to show more fully the essentially phenomenological "method" being used. At the same time I hope to indicate how Heidegger radicalizes description and thus exceeds the previous Husserlian context.

The first step is the noematic or "object-correlate" description. In this case the terminus of the correlational relation (intentional act) is observation of the horizon. As noted, this is never direct or focal in the example of the visual field, but stands at the remotest extreme from the focal center. But however vaguely, there remains the sense of horizon which may be noted in two distinct ways. First as a limit or border, (c) on the diagram, and secondly as the non-present (d) which also relates in some implicit sense to the field presence.

INTERPRETATION

Now note the language used by Heidegger in relation to horizons-phenomena. The description is appropriate and even "literal" once the phenomena are made thematic. The nearness of the horizon is that which "withdraws." And in the withdrawing the horizon is "that which goes beyond . . ." (Er übertrifft das Aussehen der Gegenstände . . .).[6] The horizon is a "going beyond" and a "passing beyond" (Ubertreffen und Uberholen).[7] Such aspects of the horizon are what may be noted at the border in its shading off into Nothing.

But while these features may be noted at the extreme periphery of the visual field as horizonal features, Heidegger wishes to take one step more and to say something about that which is nonpresent, (d). It is here that an enigma is reached. What proper descriptions may be made concerning the horizon in this sense? It is only *by relation with* that which has been previously noted that this may occur. That relation itself needs examination. However, first note the description Heidegger gives of that which exceeds the field presence. The "name" which is given is *Region* (Gegend).

But in what sense is this "name" appropriate? Region is "absent" in comparison to the field as such. Thus the description must find another means of enticing its significance. A *via negativa* may, for example, be more precise in saying what it is not than what it "is." Or, there may be some form of description which notes the *relation* only to what is present. Heidegger employs both these devices. Note the descriptions of Region: "We say that we look into the horizon. Therefore the field of vision is something open, but its openness is not due to our looking" (Wir sagen, dasz wir in den Horizont hineinsehen. Der Gesichtskreis is also in Offenes, welche Offenheit ihm nicht dadurch zukommt, dasz wir hineinsehen).[8]

The Open as such is not seen, yet it permeates the seen. It is here that beyond a "negative" detection of a horizons-phenomenon a second step is taken by way of explicating a *relation* of presence to horizons. Heidegger characterizes the openness of Region as that which *surrounds* and thus situates the visual field. "What is evident of the horizon then, is but the side facing us [the edge or border phenomenon is evident or present in an escaping mode, (c)] of an openness which surrounds us [the beyond openness (d) which is not "present" in the same way as the field]; an openness which is filled with views of the appearances of what to our re-presenting are objects" (Das Horizonthafte ist somitnur die uns zugenkehrte Seite eines uns umgebenden Offenen, das erfüllt ist mit Aussicht ins Aussehen dessen, was unserem Vorstellen als Gegenstand ercheint).[9]

It is this Openness which surrounds and situates the visual field itself which is named Region (Gegend). "It strikes me as something like a *region*, an enchanted region where everything belonging there returns to that in which it rests" (Mir kommt es so vor wie eine Gegend, durch deren Zauber alles, was ihr gehört, zu dem zurickkehrt, worin es ruht).[10] Here, however, description has reached a limit. The *strangeness* of region is proper to any form of nonpresence. Moreover, it cannot be described in simple, direct terms which would either be to reify it or to posit it as a metaphysical substance. Nevertheless, Heidegger claims, it retains a sense which allows Region to be "named". This Openness, the strangeness or enchantment, the surroundability of Region *is* descriptive in the noematic sense. But it is also description at the limits.

It is as if an extrapolation were being made. Region as the Open which surrounds field presence, area (d) of the diagram, also relates to presence and in a sense "includes" presence since (d) is an expanse which exceeds and includes (a) to (c). But (d) is not seen as such, it remains the "other side" of that which faces us. How this can be will be discussed below, for the moment the only point is to note that in Husserlian terms the first problem has been a noematic description.

In Husserlian terms, the noematic description must be supplemented by a noetic analysis of the "act" which "intends" the world terminus. If now the "noema" is this strange horizon-phenomenon of the Openness of Region, what is the "noesis" which correlates with it? Again *Gelassenheit* seems almost too simple to be true—the noesis is characterized by terms which contrast it to any form of direct, central or focal concern. (It has already been noted that horizons observation call for nonfocal exercises.) Thus Heidegger characterizes the noesis as not-willing (nicht-Wollen), releasement or letting be (Gelassenheit), and waiting (warten).

It is perhaps first important to note Heidegger explicitly indicates that these noetic "acts" are in fact correlates of horizons-phenomena. "Insofar as waiting relates to openness and openness is that-which-regions, we can say that waiting is a relation to that-which-regions." "Perhaps it is even *the* relation to that-which-regions, and in doing so lets that-which-regions reign purely as such." (Insofern es auf das Offene sich bezieht und das offene die Gegnet ist, können wir sagen, das Warten sei ein Verhältnis zur Gegnet.)[11] Again, in relation to the homely example of the visual field, now discerned to be surrounded by an Openness, a beyond, a region which situates it, what attitude or act is appropriate to this significant absence? In strictest terms there is nothing we can do to "get at it" nore can it be brought by its very located essence *into* the center of intentional awareness but must always be glimpsed from the side as it were. Thus what more appropriate or stronger, what other noetic act is there other than waiting, than openness towards what is eventually *given*? But of course when it is given it occurs *within* the presence of the region before us. The noetic description is likewise appropriate and "literal" regarding the example.

To this point I have indicated how Heidegger's description is appropriate for the paradigmatic phenomenon selected and how what first appears as odd language takes its place naturally and simply once the phenomenon is properly located. In both these respects it seems to me one can speak of Heidegger doing straightforward description in a phenomenological vein. However, there now emerges a third problem which relates to the overall interpretation of the correlation-apriori or, in Husserlian terms, to a characterization of intentionality as a constitutive process. What is the *how* of the phenomenon which is to be manifest *as* it is and *how* it is?

It is at this point that a turn must be made back to the relations within the totality of the visual field example. It is also at this point that the implications of Heideggerian radicality show themselves more fully. If now Region in the paradigm example is (d), the Open expanse which within the field is only the other side of the obscure border (c) of coming-into-presence, then Region relates as a *concealment* compared to the revealment which is present inside the visual field. In this sense it functions like the previously noted "transcendence" of objects. But now the question is not one of objects or things, but of a totality. What Heidegger is doing, it seems to me, is noting what may be termed a second set of relations within the totality of the visual example. His aim is to describe global relations between the horizon and the field of presence.

It is also here that he skirts closely to the source of metaphysics which he wishes to avoid. Thus the unusual sense of "naming" which seeks to avoid reification or objectification of Region. ". . . it lets itself be named, and being named it can be thought about." (Gleichwohl lässt es sich nennen und rennend denken . . .)[12] But what is named, Region, is not that which stands over against us and therefore does not come under the stipulation of representational or presentative experience. It is "outside" or "beyond" the very area of presence. "Probably it can't be represented at all, in so far as in representing everything has become an object that stands opposite us *within* a horizon." (Es is wohl überhaupt nicht vorzustellen, insofern durch das Vorstellen jegliches schon zum Gegenstand geworden ist, der in einem Horizont uns entgegensteht.)[13]

But now a new question can arise: if there is an essential relation within the visual field which obtains between any focal thing (a) and its situation or setting within an implicit field (b), and if it is possible to overlook or "forget" this as is apparently the case in some philosophies, is there a more radical "forgetting" which can also occur? Heidegger's answer is clearly affirmative and it is here that the second set of relations emerges. For Heidegger there is an invariant, essential relation between the horizon as Region and the entirety of the visual field (as presence). This relation is thus one between (a b)-(d). This relation may be termed the *field-horizon relation*.

Interpretation

It can be seen that this is a more expansive relation; that this relation is an extension of the first set of relations; but also that it contains an essentially different factor in that (a)-(b) relations are relations within presence and (a b)-(d) relations are between presence and non-presence. But first note the descriptions Heidegger offers for this second set of relations and the way in which they are again appropriate for the situation.

First, the relation of Region (d) to the visual field (a b) is symmetrical with the relations within (a)-(b), the Region situates and locates the field as a whole. Heidegger speaks of this as the gathering function of Region. "The region gathers, just as if nothing were happening, each to each and all into an abiding, while resting in itself. Regioning is a gathering and re-sheltering for an expanded resting in an abiding." (Die Gegend versammelt, gleich als ob sich nichts ereigne, jegliches zu jeglichem und alles zueinander in das Verweilen beim Beruhen in sich selbst. Gegnen ist das versammelnde Zurückbergen zum weiten Beruhen in der Weile.)[14]

Here the description of Region which may first be thought of as a kind of *via negativa* turns out to be something somewhat stronger. It is made by way of a set of relations discerned to obtain for the visual field. Negatively, Region is "outside" or "beyond" presence or representational knowledge. The description as openness, withdrawing, concealment, is appropriate, but not yet fully justified. The justification comes in terms of the description of the second set of relations discerned within the field presence. Region is described by what it *"does."*

The second set of relations may be clarified by referring back to a first set of "internal" relations observed within the visual field. The first set of relations are those which obtain between things and the field. There is an essential or invariant relation between any focal or core thing and the field or background within which it is situated. In terms of the diagram these are relations (a)-(b). Any thing which stands before one is always to be already situated within a wider context, a field or background, and thus does not stand alone. This (a)-(b) relation may be termed simply the *core-field relation* in terms of visual presence.

This set of relations is important for phenomenology's ability to demythologize the notion of a thing-in-itself and for all forms of simple atomism. There is here a certain isomorphism with the role of the field in respect to the thing. It, too, gathers and remains what it is in relation to the thing and remains implicit in relation to the thing. This is what Region does in relation to the whole of the visual field.

But there is a second respect in which Region also may be seen to "enter into" the field itself. Here its "appearance" is that of transcendence in respect to the thing. The thing appears as also having a hidden side, an "other" or "transcendent" side—this is the "appearance" of nonpresent horizontal phenomena within the field. "Horizon and transcendence, thus, are experienced and determined only relative to objects and our representing them." (Der Horizon und die Tranzendenz sind somit von den Gegenständen and von unserum Vorstellen aus erfahren und nur im Himblick aus die Gegenstände und unser Vorstellen bestimmt).[15]

However, as the extrapolation of relations is made, there is both a symmetry and an asymmetry between the horizon as Region and that which is within the field. In respect to the totality the openness which is the other side of horizontal presence, (c), is noted to relate back to presence in terms of what is gathered.

Thus Heidegger speaks of the openness of region as that which holds what is gathered. "It seems a region holds what comes forward to meet us; but we also said of the horizon that out of the view which it encircles, the appearance of objects comes to meet us. *If now we comprehend the horizon through the region,* we take the region itself as that which comes to meet us." (Dem Wort nach wäre die Gegend das, was uns ontgegenkommt; wir sagten doch auch vom Horizont, dass uns aus der von ihm umgrentzen Aussicht das Aussehen der Gegendstände entgegenkomme. Wenn wir jetzt den Horizont von der Gegend her fassen, nehmen wir die Gegend selbst als das uns Entgegenkommende.)[16] What Region *does*, then, is to situate, to locate, to give place to that which appears before us. But in discerning this, carefully understood, Heidegger is also claiming not to have reified, but to have correctly described in "naming", the relation between the withdrawing openness of Region and the field of presence which lies before us. In this sense Region *gives* or allows that which stands before us. And only by being open, by waiting—the only appropriate response—can we relate to what is Region. All of this is, to my mind, radically phenomenological and radically descriptive. The radicality of Heidegger lies in the discovery and use of the ratio of Region to that which rests within horizons compared to the previous descriptive ratio of an essentially Husserlian type which deals with that which lies within presence and its relations.

As a postscript I would merely add that the careful examination of a paradigm example, if it has allowed entry into the Heideggerian language, is but a first step. For just as the first phenomenological discovery of the essential relations between things and their situation in presence transforms the notion of a thing in the Husserlian sense, the *second* phenomenology which now situates and locates the field of presence—of Being, if we were to follow "Zeit und Sein"—carries with it implications of a deeper order. But at bottom the two phenomenologies are one. They call for the most radical descriptive reclamation of experience in the twentieth century.

CHAPTER NINE
Interpreting Hermeneutics: Origins, Developments and Prospects

I. The Origins of Hermeneutics

The root word for hermeneutics is the Greek verb, *hermeneuein*, which means simply in its most general meaning, *to interpret*. But definitions are abstract and to take note of the more radical origins calls for locating the concrete figures and their role for the understanding of sources. A *source*, as the French retains the sense, is the springhead, the origin from the earth itself of clear and clean water. So with *hermeneuein*. Its concrete references, as Heidegger has pointed out, ultimately point to *Hermes*, the winged messenger of the gods and, in earthly imitation, to *hermios*, who is the priest who interprets the sayings of the Oracle of Delphi, the oracle from whom Socrates claimed authority for his mission. Thus like almost every persistent and important philosophical problem in the West, hermeneutics can be traced back to the Greeks and in particular to the rise of Greek philosophy.

Hermes is the messenger of the gods, he who brings a *word* from the realm of the wordless; hermeios brings the word from the Oracle—*hermeneuein* is primordial interpretation, the bringing into word of what was previously not yet word. Hermeneutics is the most primitive sense of "to say." And from this coming to birth of word, of language, its derived meanings of explaining as in bringing to understand, and translating, as in making a foreign tongue or meaning familiar in one's own tongue, arise. By the time these root sources become philosophical in the self-conscious sense of philosophical theorizing, they mean the science or art of interpretation as per Aristotle's *Peri hermeneias,* concerning interpretation, which appears in the *Organon* along with logic, rhetoric and the analysis of all possible types of human significant utterance.

But just as most of our persistent philosophical problems have one source in Greek culture and the rise of philosophy, there is also another classical and ancient root, the Hebraic or biblical tradition. Once Greek culture became permeated, in the postclassical era, with the influx of both the Jewish and Christian traditions, hermeneutics began to take on a different significance. The biblical culture is a culture of *word,* of *Word made flesh* as the Incarnation was thought of, but more specifically of word as Word of God as expressed in a *text.* The record of the primordial word was the Bible. But the Bible was never self-evident, nor did it exist without a supporting historical context—it called for *interpretation.* To interpret, now the interpretation of a text, implies hermeneutics. And just as with the Greeks, the concrete origins in the imagery of messages from the gods became the science of interpretation, so in the post-Hellenic era hermeneutics became the science of the method of interpreting Scripture. (Exegesis was the act of interpretation in the common sense, now, while hermeneutics becomes the narrower and more theoretical "philosophy" of textual interpretation.) This meaning and the distinction which bears upon hermeneutics was amplified again at the time of the Reformation and following. No longer accepting long implicit traditions of taken-for-granted interpretation, Protestantism became self-conscious about interpretation as presumed "original" meanings were sought. Hermeneutics became the recovery of lost origins, a descent through layers of interpretation towards a pristine interpretation, the sense of "original" or primitive Christianity. Thus from the sixteenth century onward, hermeneutics becomes an essential theological enterprise.

At this point it is important to note that there is both a significant difference and a significant similarity between the meanings of hermeneutics as they occur in the two root sources of our civilization. The difference which Christian hermeneutics introduced was that hermeneutics was conceived of *narrowly,* as the theory of interpretation of texts and in particular sacred texts, and with respect to Word which had already become word. Although the word of the Bible *pointed to* the primal event, Word made flesh, it itself was already word and thus interpretation was a process *in media res*, in the midst of word.

Nevertheless, there remained in this narrower meaning of hermeneutics, a structural similarity with its Greek sense. Hermeneutics had as its task the interpretation of that which was primordial, the coming into being of Word, the *event* of meaning. Thus biblical interpretation was "archeological" in that interpretation digs back through layers of significance ever seeking some shining revelation of meaning—a word from the gods. Hermeneutics remained under the aura of Hermes, a messenger of the sacred.[1]

But the origins of hermeneutics do not cease with the melding of the two classical sources, Greek and Biblical. In modern times there has been a growing internal modification within Western culture which is all too familiar to us, the rise of the *scientific era*. We are all vaguely, but strongly aware that what counts today as truth is effected in some way or other by scientific modes of thinking. That is the case whether we are naïvely positivist and believe truth to belong solely to logical and empirical realms, or whether we are the most strongly romantic and believe that truth is precisely that which lies entirely outside of methodological verification.

This internal modification within Western culture is, on one side, an amplification of tendencies which themselves also go back to the rise of Greek philosophy. The development of the "distance" of the theoretical attitude; the valuing as true only that which is universal, lawful and orderly; and the systematic search for an ultimate coherence all was part of the original philosophical impetus. Later linked to the materialism of Democritus and Epicurus and Lucretius, this march of scientific thought branched outward from the Renaissance through the Enlightenment on to extension from one domain to another until it reached the realm of hermeneutics as well.

By the nineteenth century, scientific attitudes and methods had become partially victorious even with respect to the Bible. Although the Bible might be sacred, it must be interpreted in terms of a theory which would apply to not just sacred texts, but *any* texts. So-called "higher criticism" called for the total literary, historical and humanistic examination of all ancient texts. At the same time, the rise of the scientific era was also accompanied by another tendency, the tendency to expand the notion of a text. Earlier the Rennaissance and early Modern era saw much in the metaphor of a text in the concept of the "Book of Nature" which scientific investigation must learn to "read." Bacon's early endeavors were thus something of an early general hermeneutics of nature.

By the nineteenth century the rationalist and scientific revolution was all but final in its victory. The narrower sense of hermeneutics as a specifically theological task had to come to grasp with the wider universal claims of scientific criticism and interpretation. And it is at this junction that the contemporary sense of hermeneutics begins to take its shape. The two figures probably most responsible for this reshaping were Friedrich Schleiermacher and Wilhelm Dilthey. Without going into detail about what they theorized in particular, it is proably sufficient to note that both returned the sense of hermeneutics to its more general ancient philosophical sense, "to interpret," while also giving hermeneutics something of a new specific shape.

Schleiermacher's answer to the challenge of scientific criticism and thinking was basically to *accommodate* it into the theological task itself. Biblical hermeneutics must be transformed into a *general* hermeneutics, universal in scope and valid for the wider problems of interpretation. With Schleiermacher, hermeneutics became the *philosophical* science of understanding itself. The principles of hermeneutics were to be understood as basic to any kind of textual and historical interpretation whatsoever and biblical interpretation became but one instance of an area of interpretation. Hermeneutics, with Schleiermacher, became humanistic—but also it became broad in its ancient sense as the art or science of interpretation as such. However, in the humanistic direction, hermeneutics was now linked to the problem of human and historical understanding.

Dilthey followed Schleiermacher in a somewhat more specific and less theological direction. He saw hermeneutics as the possible foundation for a science of human and historical dimensions, what we would today call the behavioral and social sciences or human sciences. As a science of historical, human understanding, hermeneutics was to enunciate the principles which would differentiate the human or social sciences from the natural sciences. And thus the debate between "understanding" and "explanation" was entered.

The emerging contemporary sense of hermeneutics, then, is one which refers particularly to the interpretation of the human and by the end of the nineteenth century one might already say that hermeneutics was the latent *existential* science.

Were one to follow linearly the progression of the history of the use and transformation of hermeneutics, the next logical step would be to turn directly to contemporary hermeneutic philosophers—but to do so would sidestep the single largest *indirect* development underlying contemporary hermeneutics. That is the development of *phenomenology* and in particular the phenomenology of Edmund Husserl. It is at this juncture that a number of perennial philosophical issues arise.

II. Phenomenology and the Transformation of Hermeneutics

Husserl's problems and their sources, at first, seem rather far removed from those of either classical or early contemporary hermeneutics. Rather, Husserl's concerns for a radical reformulation of the sciences, arose within the traditions of Modern rationalism and empiricism. The ideal—the dream—of Modern philosophy had been for a truly radical beginning, a search for some absolute grounding from which to build, step by step, a certain and universal science. And whether this was the innate, clear and distinct ideas of the cogito of Descartes, or the simple ideas of Locke at the origins of empiricism, this search was also Husserl's. Husserl's phenomenology was the search for yet another absolute grounding for a universal science. And the language used by

Husserl remained under the aura of his philosophical roots. The "transcendental ego," "transcendental subjectivity," his "science of experience," with its "descriptive psychology," "apodicticity," all retain the flavor of the transcendental traditions of Modern philosophy.

But the methods he evolved in the process soon threatened to break the old language and the old concepts as well. It remains Husserl's fate to have begun a revolution which soon outstripped him, but which must remain dependent upon him for many of its essential insights.

To note the philosophical interest in the relationship of phenomenology and hermeneutics, a preliminary observation about Husserl's strategy must be noted: As I have already pointed out, Husserl's problematic arose and took shape within the already constituted language and terminology of transcendental philosophy with its "subject" and "object" and its problem of how knowledge is constituted. On the explicit level Husserl took up this language and addressed himself to the set problems of this tradition. Yet implicitly almost every struggle Husserl had with the tradition and, for that matter, with himself, pointed in another direction. In fact, often the results of the struggle pointed in directions exactly opposite to those which had been held by the tradition itself.

Perhaps the best example of this strategy and the problems it created may be seen from Husserl's famous *Cartesian Meditations*. The *Cartesian Meditations* were the mature development from a set of lectures Husserl delivered in Paris, in an attempt to interest French thinkers in phenomenology. The strategy employed, partly apologetic, party polemic, was to utilize the explicit model of Descartes's version of philosophical method with its notion of "doubt," a reduction by analysis to "clear and distinct ideas," and the establishment of the "ego cogito" as a base, served as both the model and foil for Husserl's own phenomenology. On the one hand, phenomenology was portrayed as being "like" Cartesian philosophy with its own method of "suspension" as a modification of "doubt," its own analysis into clear and distinct "givens" of intuition as a modification of geometrical method, and into its own version of the subject as "transcendental subjectivity." But on the other hand, in and through each of these similarities, phenomenology arrived at conclusions directly contrary to those found in Cartesian philosophy. What phenomenological "suspension" showed was *the ultimate indubitability of the World;* what the analysis showed was that *"givens" are in fact constituted* by a complex process and not simples; and what "subjectivity" revealed ultimately was the *intersubjectivity* of the transcendental.

In general, some version of this strategy is followed in all of Husserl's mature writings. He begins with what is (seemingly) familiar, accepting it in a provisional way, but also undercutting it by placing it in "brackets," as an object to be examined and taken apart from a new and different perspective. In this process, the layers of the (seemingly) given object are unlayered so that both the object and the process by which the object is constituted are discovered. Here is a latent archeology—a *hermeneutic* process—which deconstructs what was previously taken for granted.

But such a process contains an inherent flaw. By taking what is (seemingly) familiar, situated in an already developed language with its accompanying terminology, the choice is one which allows the nonneutrality of the already developed language to retain its strength in spite of the attempted deconstruction through phenomenology. This unwanted and unexpected result plagued Husserl during his working life and remains extant in what to my mind are the still present misunderstandings of Husserl. Critics of his phenomenology still cry that this method is "subjectivistic," that it is a revived "idealism," that its domain extends no farther than "psychology," and the like, in spite of Husserl's intention to avoid precisely each of these epithets.

In this respect, Husserl must be termed a *naïve* hermeneut. He did develop a powerful archeology of meaning in and through his "phenomenological reductions," but he failed to avoid, or transcend, or cut through the universe of discourse which retained its power through and in spite of his attempts to overcome it, precisely because he was not able to neutralize the nonneutral themes which pervaded the language of Modern philosophy.

Husserl's hermeneutically oriented followers were quick to discover this weakness and promptly attempted to overcome this strategy. Martin Heidegger, at least as early as *Being and Time*, was keenly aware of Husserl's strategic weakness and while adapting what I have elsewhere argued is a quite explicit phenomenological method for his own fundamental ontology, also sharply diverged from Husserl's linguistic naïveté. Viewed in one way, Heidegger's strategy was to avoid as thoroughly as possible the extant problems of Modern philosophy by coining a radically new language which skirted or circumvented the terminology of "subject"-"object" and the constitution of knowledge. Heidegger "existentialized" each of the Husserlian steps, still following the Husserlian method quite clearly, but substituted a new sense at each stage. "Intentionality," which was Husserl's term for the essential correlation between the subject and his world, became "Being-in-the-World"; Husserl's "ego," transcendental or otherwise, became "Dasein" with the specific etymologically literal sense of being-here (being-there). The relationship between Dasein and World was no longer solely or even primarily a *knowledge* relationship, but a matter of existential dimensions, "existentials." I shall return to these modifications in more detail in a moment, but here I would like to underline the essentially different and more self-aware linguistic strategy employed by Heidegger, the radical hermeneut.

This radical Heideggerian strategy, also reverberates in an interesting way with the Ordinary Language strategies of the contemporary era. The "new" language which he coins is in, one sense, only new to philosophy. He sidesteps the usual terminology of Modern philosophy by turning to ancient, revived or even literalizations inherent in ordinary language. Clearly Heidegger's language is not ordinary—but it is from the wealth of human history and language that he derives a richness lacking in Husserl and in much technically constructed philosophy.

Paul Ricœur, another follower of Husserl, draws from a different strategy with respect to the transformation of transcendental phenomenology to hermeneutic phenomenology. He criticizes Heidegger's approach as too "direct." The new language world created by Heidegger, Ricœur claims, too quickly cuts off the debate with classical issues (indeed, that is precisely what it was meant to do in one respect). Nor can one viably maintain Husserl's "idealism" or naïveté about the subject. Rather one must create a *dialectic,* a debate in which two views may be interrogated and a gradual approximation of terms occur such that the new meanings, a "third term," may arise from within the debate. Ricœur's is a restorative hermeneutic.

There is a second and equally important issue in the movement from Husserl to his main hermeneutic followers (for our purposes here Heidegger and Ricœur), which bears notice: There is a shift in what is taken to be of primary importance with respect to perception and language between Husserl and the hermeneuts. If Husserl borrowed from Modern rationalism its language of "subject," "ego" and the like, he borrowed the basically perceptualist notion of primordial evidence from the empiricists. Perception was the place where "primordial dator evidence" arises.

Both Heidegger and Ricœur shift from this emphasis: Heidegger specifically maintains in *Being and Time* that perception becomes what it is only with respect to the fundamental contexts of language and discourse, and Ricœur finds that all experience is already mediated *in media res,* in a world of symbols and myths and their interpretation.

The hermeneutic motto that "Man *is* language" expresses in part this shift from a perceptualist to a "linguistic" phenomenology. It also takes on its specific positive quality in contemporary hermeneutics.

However, in this context it is important to take some initial note of the specific contributions made by Husserl for the transformation of contemporary hermeneutics and its existential philosophy of language. These contributions may be made most clear, it seems to me, if one begins, not with Husserl's involuted strategies, but with the actual *results* of his phenomenology and with the key notions understood in terms of their *functions.*

The key notion in Husserl's phenomenology, around which everything else revolves, is *intentionality.* On the explicit (and therefore shallow) level of understanding, intentionality is simply the referential or directed nature of consciousness. All consciousness,

Interpretation

Husserl says over and over, is consciousness of _____. Thus to perceive is to perceive something; to love is to love something; to imagine is to imagine something, etc. This level of the interpretation of intentionality is simply that of a descriptive psychology of conscious processes. But that is neither the ultimate significance of intentionality, nor does it reveal its true phenomenological function. At its depth, intentionality may be described as the *foundational correlational rule* of phenomenology by which any area of possible knowledge whatsoever is located and circumscribed.

In the deep sense of intentionality, the notion is neither psychological nor even strictly epistemological—it is ontological, the condition of the possibility of there being either "subject" or "object" or, for that matter, "world." Subject and object arise within what Husserl sometimes calls the *correlation-apriori* which began as intentionality.

In simplest terms, this means that intentionality as a primitive rule, a correlational rule, takes account of the interrelatedness and interdependence of what in the Modern tradition has been called "subject" and "object." Neither term makes sense in and of itself and neither term can, in fact, be dealt with in isolation from the other. The whole of Husserlian philosophy revolves around this central correlation scheme, although the terminology and refinements upon how the correlation is to be understood vary from period to period. Take note of just two instances of how the ontological correlation occurred in Husserl's work:

First, there is the early correlation of what Husserl called "noema" and "noesis." Put most simply, "noema" is *that* which is experienced, the *what* of experience, the "object-correlate." "Noesis" is the way in which the what is experienced, the experiencing or act of experiencing, the "subject-correlate." Thus, no "noema" without "noesis" (there is nothing which is present *as evidenced* unless it is present to experience) and there is no "noesis" without a "noema" (no act of experience without that towards which it is directed.) One may formalize this relation thusly:

$$\text{noesis} \longrightarrow \text{noema.}$$

Later, Husserl was to complicate this bare scheme with his "egology" and make of the correlation a three-part correlation as in the *Cartesian Meditations*. There Husserl retained the sense of correlation, but added to the act of experiencing a specific carrier of the act, the "ego." In this form the correlation took the form:

ego-cogito-cogitatum.

In the basic transformation from Cartesian philosophy, this form of the correlation was one which maintained the essential insight of the earlier version of the correlation: no activity of experience (cogito as active, the thinking of the ego,) without something which is thought (the cogitatum). The "addition" is the ego itself as that which does the thinking. But in essence, with or without an ego, the correlation remains functionally the same.

The results of using such a correlation analysis, Husserl himself did not fully apprehend—at least as those who followed him did. For the implications of the correlation for the traditions of Modern philosophy are quite radical. These may be pointed up most drastically by contrasting them with the taken-for-granted conclusions of the Cartesian tradition.

First, on the side of the "object-correlate," for phenomenology there can be no such thing as a "worldless" subject. Doubt may be cast upon how to interpret the world, *i.e.*, the question remains open as to whether the world is basically "material" or "mental" or whatever may be the case in the metaphysical tradition, but *that* there is a world as that which is constantly present to experience cannot be doubted. There is a constant presence of something that is "there," whether it is the construction of a demon or the creation of a god or the eternally given accidental matter of the universe. The world sense is primordially the sense of phenomenological presence and *is as indubitable as the ego.*

Secondly, on the side of the "subject-correlate" there is a negative result. There is no "subject" without a world, but neither is there any immediately self-transparent subject. The subject, within the phenomenological correlation, is deprived of its singular immediacy and of its presumed self-evidence. Positively put, *the subject now can know itself only by means of the world.* This implication of the correlation was, I believe, never fully grasped by Husserl himself, but was grasped quickly by both Heidegger and Ricœur, not in contrast to the trajectory of phenomenology, but in keeping with that trajectory.

Husserl already knew, from his investigations, that phenomenologically one must *begin* with the world, the noema, that which appeared and from that work back *reflexively* to the subject, the noesis, the act of experience which is indicated by and through the world. That is, the shape of the experience is indicated by the way in which that which is experienced shows itself. Thus in the primitive correlation an order of procedure is established such that the noematic analysis must precede the noetic analysis (as per the diagram):

Noesis   noema
(2) ⟶ (1)
⟵ - - - -

The noesis, the act of experiencing, is not oly "second" in the order of analysis—it is known only *reflexively*.

But because Husserl had adapted the already traditional metaphysical framework of "layers" in which there was to be an ultimate ground, he presumed that that which was arrived at ultimately in terms of the *order* of the analysis must be that which was fundamental. This was the source of his so-called "idealism." If we use the second form of the correlation, the founding stratum becomes the ego itself:

ego-cogito-cogitatum
(3) ⟵ (2) ⟵ (1)

Here the order proceeds from the cogitatum, reflexively (backwards) towards the ego which Husserl took to be the ultimate, founding stratum. He did not so clearly note the implicit limitation and darkness which his correlation and its reflexively placed upon the ego.

Heidegger and Ricœur *did* recognize this implication. And each in his own way turned phenomenology towards hermeneutics. First, let us take very brief note of the way in which Heidegger adapted almost entirely the Husserlian functional model of analysis in *Being and Time*.

Functionally, the Heideggerian analytic of Dasein operates exactly like Husserl's primary correlation. In this case the overall correlation looks like this:

(Dasein) being-in-the-World.

Recall that the preliminary task of *Being and Time* is to analyze the being of one being, Dasein, which is the kind of being we ourselves are. But to accomplish this task, Heidegger like Husserl and unlike Cartesian philosophy and its accompanying tradition, turns first to the World. Indeed, what must come first for Heidegger is a clarification of the "worldhood of the world." Dasein is to be uncovered in terms of its world. In short, Dasein is not to be known "directly," but "indirectly," by means of its world. Here we have the same form as the Husserlian analysis:

(Dasein) being-in-the-World.
(3)◄——— (2)◄——— (1)

But while the correlation and the order of analysis is isomorphic with Husserl's analysis of intentionality, there are two major modifications in the Heideggerian version of the correlation.

First, every element in the analysis has been "existentialized," that is, interpreted as components and structures of existence, rather than "merely" of psychology and epistemology. The formal ontology of Husserl has been replaced with a fundamental or "material" ontology in Heidegger. Secondly, Dasein, that to be analysed, not only is the last term in the order, but must be uncovered through the process of the *interpretation* of the phenomena, reflexively, but now a reflection specifically termed hermeneutic. That is why in this case I have placed a parenthesis around Dasein. Dasein has become enigmatic. And as the world of Dasein changes, so does Dasein.

Interpretation

In addition to the two modifications from the Husserlian base, one other addition specifically relevant to the hermeneutic direction given to phenomenology by Heidegger may be noted at this point. "Being-in as such," Heidegger's term for the correlation itself, is broken down into three equiprimordial dimensions: State of mind, understanding, and discourse. These are the primordial ways in which Dasein is related to World. Note with the primacy of *understanding* and *discourse* one might already say that this primary relationship is one which is already *language*. Language *is* being-in, or, language, existentially, is what constitutes the peculiar and particular character of our being-here. To analyse Dasein is to analyze language in its existential sense.

Thus for Heidegger one can say "Man is language," or, to invert the idea, one can note that language is a way, a mode of being in the world.

Paul Ricœur, in a more indirect way, affirms the same direction towards a hermeneutic philosophy. In contrast to Heidegger, Ricœur retains the language of the subject and remains in the center of the debates about how self-knowledge is constituted. His strategy is to develop a dialectic between phenomenology and some other, usually "objectivist" strategy. Each of the nonphenomenological strategies is seen to *limit* the pretensions of Husserlian naïveté, on the methodological level, and the pretensions of the ego, on the ontological level. For Ricœur it is not only the case that the ego is known only reflexively, there is also a temptation to self-deception and narcissism on the part of the subject to avoid authentic self-knowledge.

Of particular interest are the recent analyses of Ricœur found in his *Freud and Philosophy* and *The Conflict of Interpretations*. In these book Ricœur interrogates a whole series of what he calls "hermeneutics of suspicion," interpretations of the self which dethrone and cast into doubt the claims of both Cartesian self-transparency and any direct form of self-knowledge. Ricœur sees what amounts to the whole "Hegelian left" and subsequently influenced methods as constituting a common strategy of attempts to pierce through "false consciousness." Nietzsche, Marx, and primarily Freud, each find ways to break through the pretensions of the ego and find what is presumably unexpected, underlying various surface manifestations. Moreover, each employs a basically "linguistic" strategy in which there is some underlying "different" meaning to be brought out of some innocuous or even seemingly contrary surface manifestation. To cite one familiar example: Freudian analysis sees in *The Psychopathology of Daily Life,* not accidents or neutral significance to jokes and slips of the tongue, but expressions of deeply held "unconscious" attitudes and beliefs. Ricœur, in his hermeneuticizing of Freud, sees in this theory, not an accurate metaphysics of the self (the machinery of super-ego, ego, id), but a sophisticated linguistic strategy which elicits the "grammar of desire." The implication for phenomenology, at least in its naïve Husserlian sense, is that *more is meant than is intended in each expression,* and thus a hermeneutic process is needed to explicate the unsaid.

But in a deeper sense, Ricœur has developed precisely one of the latent implications of Husserl's reflexive correlation. The subject does not and cannot know itself simply in Husserl's sense either. It knows itself in terms of its world, its "Other." In the psychoanalytic situation a specific and dramatic instance of such reflexivity occurs. The patient slowly and painfully learns *through* an other, the analyst. It is the analyst who brings out and allows to be made present for self-discovery, the hidden meanings and surplus meanings which the patient himself or herself and by himself or herself did not and could not discover. Ultimately, for all phenomenology, subjectivity *is* intersubjectivity, but it is never that *immediately.* The radical decentering which occurs in the various "hermeneutics of suspicion" point to the difficulty of this process. But the process itself is essentially hermeneutic, an ongoing interpretation.

Ricœur has taken this idea specifically into the notion of a *text.* And in his even more recent works, *La Métaphor Vive,* for example, what reemerges is once again an affirmation of what was latent for hermeneutics in the Husserlian correlation. What is it to understand a text? I believe I can point to one illustration which simultaneously shows both how Ricœur reaffirms the phenomenological correlation and relates to a standard problem of interpretation.

The so-called "intentional fallacy," which holds the impossible ideal for understanding a text by means of understanding the author's intentions, would be and is repudiated by Ricœur essentially phenomenological hermeneutic. Just as the "subject" is not known either first or by itself in Husserlian phenomenology, neither can it be so known in textual analysis. Rather, what is presented is the "world" of the text. That is the matter to be understood first. To be sure, a "world" may show—indirectly—something of the author, even something of the author which the author may not have known directly about himself, but whatever is known or can be found out, occurs here reflexively, by means of the "world" of the text.

For Ricœur, as for Heidegger, "Man is language." But language is enigmatic, often equivocal, and always multi-dimensioned. This is so for the subject as well and in this, language is "like" the self.

In this brief and at best schematic glimpse at the impact of phenomenology upon hermeneutics, I have concentrated only on one central set of problems, the central notion of intentionality and its transformation into the ontology of being-in-the-world, with its related problems of world and self as they unfold within a hermeneutic investigation.

I have suggested that a founding dimension of being-in-the-world is seen by hermeneutic phenomenologists as discourse or language. Thus language is neither something merely "inside us" nor "outside" us, but is an *existentiale*. This is why Heidegger can speak of language as the "house of being" and of "language speaking" (*Sprache spricht.*)

But before turning to the last task in this essay, please take note of the connection between the hermeneutic philosophers and the earlier problems and traditions I left in the nineteenth century. The "general hermeneutics" of Schliermacher with the primary task of developing an account of historical understanding overall, and the *Wissenschaften* problem of understanding in Dilthey as a foundation for the social-historical sciences, is in effect continued by Heidegger and Ricœur. Phenomenology has provided a rigorous methodology, neither "subjectivistic" nor "objectivistic" by which to approach social, historical, human phenomena. Moreover, in its hermeneutic guise it takes as its focal dimension, language in its deepest existential significance. The prospect for phenomenological hermeneutics lies in its own development of the philosophy of language.

III. Prospects for Hermeneutic Phenomenology

The philosophical focus of phenomenological hermeneutics, then, is an existential philosophy of language. In turn, an existential philosophy of language returns to the most ancient hermeneutic tradition. Hermes and the Christ signify a movement from the wordless to word and the hermeneutic philosophy of language has turned to the problem of the "birth of meaning."

Poetry, as Heidegger conceives it, is primordial word. It is a "saying" which allows Being to be seen. *Poiesis* is creative-uncovering word which lets Being "shine forth." And poetic word, that which is most ancient, is united with that which is most radically futural. Such a word is "horizontal" in the phenomenological sense. This is to say that the coming into being of meaning becomes the focus for a hermeneutic philosophy of language.

Ricœur has exactly the same vector in his thought. His long Hegira towards the "poetics of the will" through the sciences of language center on the analysis of equivocity and ultimately *polysemy*. Poetic word, most dramatically apparent in symbols and myths, is the richness of polysemic language. But language itself in any word has this possibility. It is the productive imagination which enhances this polysemy and it is to the imagination that Ricœur has turned today. Hope, Ricœur's leading religious idea, takes its shape through the imagination of the possible in poesis. Thus Ricœur's philosophy of language, too, centers upon the poetic with a restorative and projective trajectory.

Both Heidegger and Ricœur retain the thought of a coming-into-meaning symbolized by the ancients and revived by the Romantics in the motto of Johann Georg Hamann, "Poetry is the mother tongue of language."

Ours is, however, a very unromantic era and the question arises:

is a search for a word from Hermes or a recognition of Word made flesh possible in the late twentieth century? The gods, it would seem, have long since lapsed into silence and even the notion of a sacred text has fallen into the relativity of a plurality of "religious utterances." Does "language speak" for contemporary hermeneutics?

I do not intend these vast questions to lead to a long meditation, but I do wish to suggest a few quite concrete problems which maintain the restorative-projective trajectory of hermeneutic philosophy in the present.

I should like to suggest that a "first word," the "birth of meaning," "poiesis," fixes not something which is exclusively "then" or "yet to come," but that its secrets are mundane and lie amongst us. Restoratively, one task of an existential philosophy of language is to recollect for us an understanding of the ways in which human discourse, speech, is *embodied,* the way meaning becomes flesh.[2] Projectively, this same task is one which must take into account the genuinely new embodiments of language which encompass us today. I think this includes, as only Heidegger in this tradition saw clearly, the question of technology as a hermeneutic problem. On the surface it may seem strange to link these two lines of thought, but underneath it seems to me that hermeneutic phenomenology demands that they belong together.

Our era, as philosophers have intuitively known, must necessarily come to grips with language precisely because language in contemporary times has exploded in a double sense. Language has become both a saturation of "languages," not only native tongues, but new tongues, and it has become newly incarnated in ways never known to humans in previous times.

It is true that ordinary discourse in a native tongue remains the coin of everyday life. But in a megasocietal and megatechnological world we all learn multiple "tribal languages" of the techniques which our various scientific and academic "tribes" bring into being. Nor is this explosion limited to ordinary and technical "languages"; it has burgeoned into a whole series of "artificial" or constructed languages such as those of mathematics, the symbolic logics and various computer languages. And even if we do not "speak" or "read" such languages, we must live under their aura.

Additionally, the way speech now becomes embodied no longer is restricted to that which is face-to-face or to listening and direct voice. Instead, we have amplified and extended our listening and voice through telephones, radios, and the current popular CB. Writing, the ancient nonverbal language of texts which posed an ancient hermeneutic problem, is now adumbrated with the equally transformed spatial-temporal reproductions of cinema, television and tape recorder. As of yet there is no full hermeneutic investigation of this series of embodiments. These new "texts" call for new types of hermeneutics.

This explosion of language into "languages" with its accompanying diffusion into technological embodiments saturates and changes our "World." And if phenomenological ontology is correct, when one correlate (the world) changes it implies a change in the other (ourselves) but this change can only be understood by understanding the change in the "World."

I therefore suggest that contemporary hermeneutics in its trajectory of restoration-projection may both focus upon the re-collective moment which recalls the primitive sense of incarnate speech and anticipate the futural sense of extended speech.

In the restorative moment, incarnate speech is focally and nominatively that which is face-to-face and is primarily embodied in heard and spoken word.

Richard Palmer in his book on *Hermeneutics* points out this simple but primary phenomenon which gets overlooked:

> . . . interpretation is a form of saying. Likewise, *oral* saying or singing is an interpretation. In Greek times, *hermeneia* could refer to an oral recitation, of Homer for instance . . . through his intonations (he) "interprets" him, conveying more than he realizes or understands. He thus becomes, like Hermes, a vehicle for Homer's message.[3]

And in relation to the biblical root of hermeneutics:

> . . . the Bible is not information; it is a message, a "proclamation," and was meant to be read aloud, meant to be heard.[4]

Thus, Palmer concludes:

> (Hermeneutics) has led us back to the primordial form and function of language as living sound filled with the power of meaningful utterance. Language, as it emerges from nonbeing, is not signs, but sound.[5]

What Palmer points to is the primitive embodiment of language. Speech is sounded and sound is neither neutral nor reducible to a single layer of determined meaning. The "birth of meaning" lies in the *speech event* and its normative embodiment is as a phenomenon of silence, listening and sound. There is always more than information in spoken word.

Yet the very formulation of the contemporary sciences of language skew our observations in a different direction. Rather than a phenomenological emphasis upon word made flesh, the linguistic sciences divide the speech act into the two regions of meaningless sound (acoustics, and related sciences) and into formal disembodied semiologies (semiology, semantics, grammar and the like). Moreover, by taking such a turn, the temptation is to model language more and more upon the notion of "information."

A phenomenological hermeneutic in its restorative moment must, among other things, restore the sense of the normative embodiment of language in the concrete discourse of listening and voice. It must rediscover the nonneutral and rich significance of "musical" word.

But the dialogue of face to face, while primitive and normative, is clearly not the only manifestation of language for contemporary humans. Increasingly, language is extended in technological mediations. Television, cinema, telephone, and a whole array of language and language-related instrumentation transforms the texture of our ordinary life-world. Time and space take on different significations as "objective" or "geographical" and even "temporal" distances become collapsed into the near-distance of instant or repeated communication. As Heidegger rightly claimed, technology is in fact a kind of being. It can better be understood in the sense of a language-analogue than as a thing-analogue. Here, too, I see a task for a hermeneutically oriented philosophy. One which must deal with the projective possibilities of a technological civilization in which language no longer is discourse on the model of the face to face. Such a projection cannot remain satisfied with the paradigm of immediate discourse, but must revert to the other side of hermeneutics, the notion of the text through which past worlds become known to us.

Only now interpretation of a text across past temporal distance cannot remain the only direction for contemporary hermeneutics. It must also turn to the "possible worlds" of the future. Such an exploration in a radical sense, of the imaginative hopes and possibilities of humankind—and particularly those becoming horizontal in technological society—is called for as a prospect for hermeneutics. I am calling for not only interpretation across the past, but across the future, in which one concrete and necessary task is the "science fiction" of a possible hermeneutic. In short, the projective hermeneutics is one which looks at "texts" across possible futures, the futures made available in technological culture.

The double movement, already begun in Heidegger and Ricœur, may continue in such prospects, for of hermeneutics there is no end.

CHAPTER TEN

Phenomenology and Deconstructive Strategy

I. Introduction

Rhetoric is the weaponry of the internecine wars which scholars wage. And on the field of contemporary intellectual battlegrounds the heavy artillery has been brought out by the newly emergent army of post-structuralist deconstructionists. As the newest invaders they have drawn defensive fire on several fronts. In literary critical circles the battlecries have been those between "humanists" and "deconstructionists," with the former decrying the abandonment of what is perceived as both the objective task of criticism and its moral obligation, and the latter characterizing all forms of previous criticism as old fashioned and out of date.

The same, often effective, rhetoric is employed against what historically may be considered a former ally, phenomenology. And it is to this particular battle that I shall attend here. Phenomenologists, having barely established a beachhead in the still ongoing struggle with philosophical analysis, suddenly find themselves attacked from the rear by a new wave of deconstructionists. What many generals in the phenomenological army thought to have been their major weapons, for example, the "self" in ontology and "expression" in language, have had them declared eliminated or out-of-date by the newer invaders. The newer weaponry, acquired from semiology and combined with a kind of post-structuralist reduction strategy, is proclaimed to successfully deconstruct what is taken for Reality, the "text."

I have deliberately chosen the metaphor of warfare for this

introduction because in a strict analogue to war, intellectual battles do change the face of the world—but not always in expected ways and certainly not always in terms of who wins battles. Deeper and below the levels of military campaigns lie cultural and economic forces which have the longer reaching effects. Historically it is probably the case that as many invaders have ended up being captured, or at least modified, by the cultures of those invaded as the other way around. There are probably as many invasions which deeply penetrated continents whose effects vanished with little trace as there are of those which changed the direction of subsequent history. Thus, beyond the immediate rhetorical explosions, we must also seek to gain a sense of what deeper possibilities there might be for the ultimate outcome of the current conflict.

I propose to analyze the current battle by beginning at ground level with a quick look at several of the issues which separate the immediate combatants, phenomenology and deconstructionism, and then ascend to observe the array from a higher altitude so as to discern several larger issues. The ascent will take notice of the larger force which still occupies the highlands, analytic philosophy of language, so that the comparative strategies of all three forces might be seen. Once this is accomplished, I shall redescend and undertake a more precise strategic analysis of those elements of phenomenology in particular which reciprocate most deeply with a semiotically based deconstructionism.

While the ultimate goal of warfare is victory, diplomats known that continuous war impoverishes the land, and thus we hope that moments of peace might allow agriculture, commerce and art to flourish. It may turn out that the deeper reciprocities are such that apparent enemies are more thoroughly interlocked than they might consider in the heat of battle.

II. Phenomenology and Deconstructionism

At ground level the phenomenological army stands behind a battleflag which carries the motto, "to the things themselves." Often cited, this motto does implicitly contain an entire phenomenological program. First, there must be *Things*. And in spite of the fact that the founder of phenomenology characterized his philosophical position as transcendental idealism, there remained within the diverse development of phenomenology (into existentialist and hermeneutic forms) a kind of *realist* emphasis. In its earliest Husserlian form one detects that the Thing retains something of the sense of a real perceptual object, a material object, at least as the model of comparison for other entities. To be sure, the taken-for-granted thing is rapidly transformed into the phenomenologically present thing—and that transformation remains essential throughout the transmutations of phenomenology. However, it remains the referendum of the phenomenological process. Writ large and reinterpreted as a totality, it is the World and it is always the World with which phenomenology begins and from which the descriptive analysis springs. The World retains its sense of realism which precisely separates phenomenology from the earlier subjectivism implicit in modern metaphysics, whether Cartesian or empiricist.

Heidegger, in existentializing Husserl, retained at the level of strategy, the same realist emphasis. The thing in Heidegger does undergo another transformation. It loses its primacy as a material object insofar as that object belongs to the disinterestedly perceived standing bits of the universe which modern metaphysics took as primary, and became in Heidegger the World which is revealed through human action. But the reason for this change may be found directly within the trajectory of phenomenology. Yet, in spite of this seemingly radical reinterpretation of Husserl, phenomenology must begin its analysis with the noematic or object-correlate, so Heidegger's *Being and Time* looks first at the Worldhood of the World.

What the motto does not express directly, however, became the second but more important issue in the new battle situation. The "things themselves," unlike objects in classical realisms, do not stand alone or independent from the entity to whom they are present—the ego, the self, Dasein, the experiencer. Note, however, that the very implicitness of a subject is also different from classical transcendental positions.

Husserl's first interpretation of this situation was one which focused experience in a subject, an *ego*. Just as the ego-centered consciousness and the thing, at base, retained a classical perceptualist significance, so the subject's primary access to the world was modeled upon perception. However, in contrast to classical transcendental positions, Husserl's ego is arrived at indirectly or reflexively, by way of the World. Noematic analysis precedes noetic analysis. Nevertheless, once arrived at, the ego becomes the "primitive" of Husserl's system. The ego, while not creating the World, nevertheless *constitutes* it.

Heidegger's *Being and Time* repeats and reinterprets this strategy. It is from the Worldhood of the World that Heidegger reflexively arrives at those activities of Dasein which allow the World to be present in the way it is for humans: through moods, understanding and discourse. Thus in both Husserl and Heidegger there is retained a kind of realism of the World and a concretist interpretation of a human subject as experiencer of the World. Put most simply, phenomenology attempts in some way to descriptively analyze Things and The World by means of analyzing the full range of human experience.

What, then, of the newcomers, the deconstructionists? If one believes their deliberately aimed rhetoric, we suddenly have a battlefield in which one army still carries battleflags and handheld weapons (*Vorhandenheit*?), while the other appears with a self-automated set of Darth Vader laser machinery (the language of "automatic writing," "literary" and "conceptual machines" does permeate some of the more extreme deconstructionist prose). Certainly one immediately notes the absence of Things, World and a Self (or are they merely hidden?) appearing in their battle array.

At the level of tactics it might be said that the most explicit attack made by post-structuralism was upon the notion of self which, once dispersed at the least, or eliminated at the most, served to allow its correlates, Thing and World, to disappear as well. In general the implication is that by turning from phenomena to semiotic differences which change over time, the notions of "self," "thing" and "world" are taken to be "invented" within a particular slice of semiotic time. Thus Foucault can speak of the "invention" of Man, Freedom, etc. The rhetorical implication is, of course, that once this is seen we have put out of play the residual realism of now surpassed phenomenology.

Even initially I should like to take note of a certain irony in the use of this tactic precisely because it is one which should be familiar to any practicing phenomenologist! From the very beginnings of Husserlian phenomenology the famed machinery of *epochē*, the reductions, and the gestalt switch from a "natural" to a "phenomenological" attitude could be interpreted as a heuristic device to get one to see "phenomenologically."[1] Then, once the new perspective was gained, it could be said that one no longer needed to bother with the complexities of the machinery.[2] Now the post-structuralists might be said to be using a similar device precisely to decenter what they conceive of as the residual realism retained by phenomenology. The shift to a semiological perspective is in some sense a gestalt shift equivalent to the previous shift formulated by phenomenology, and as with duck-rabbits, when the duck is seen the rabbit disappears and vice-versa.

Following any profound shift in perspective, there is an equivalent shift in what constitutes a problem.[3] Hypothesize here a dissipation of a critical problem: the old hermeneutic questions of an intentional fallacy. In baldest terms within contemporary deconstructionism one might simply point out that no-subject/no-intentional fallacy. Put another way, once the locus of meaning is shifted, dispersed as it were among the elements of a semiotic web, so also is dissipated any author's simple intention with respect to possible meaning.

To this point I have been dwelling upon what has disappeared from the deconstructionist armory. What replaces the displaced pheomena should be of equal interest. In taking this look, I deliberately want to select the more avant-garde, extreme and perhaps outrageous examples of deconstructionism and its effects. Recent Derrida will do.

Take a text: If one views a text (perceptually) it usually appears first as writing which is centered on the page, surrounded by margins, but the focal center is clearly the bulk of what is written. Then, if one reads the text, what usually emerges as focal is what the text is about, however complex that may be, as indeed any

INTERPRETATION

text usually is. What does Derrida do with a text? Posed in the way I have indicated, he immediately decenters what seems to be focal and immediate. His focus is radically shifted to titles, signatures, margins, borders, divisions, etc. In short, he draws our attention to features which are there, but usually taken at most as background, secondary or unimportant features.

In a sense this is a highly "phenomenological" technique. For example, in an analysis of perception, phenomenologists like to point out that while what stands out (figures) are usually most obvious because they are the referenda of our usual perceptions, all figures take their position upon a background which is equally present and which constitutes the field of perceivability. In short, this move "decenters" focal perception so as to attend to taken-for-granted but important fringe features. Similarly, to point out that all perceptions include not only manifest surfaces, but latent "backsides," is to "decenter" at least the usual interpretations *of* perception. I am suggesting that this device—perhaps taken to Niezschean excess—is a familiar ploy of Derrida. Indeed, one can see, once the operation is known, how to follow along with such deconstructions. (Is there a Derrida text which addresses itself to the empty background of the page? If not, there ought to be.)

Once the focus is decentered, however, a second more radical step is taken. In the Derrididean tactic this seems to be a kind of playfulness which then wants to read the fringe back into the center as a kind of shadow presence. This tactic appeared early in the assertion of the primacy of writing in *On Grammatology* and *Writing and Difference*. If writing "precedes" speech (decentering the subject), its "evidence" is the *trace* which must be found but since the trace is not obvious the finding calls for a kind of play. Similarly in "late" Derrida, the margins, signatures and borders get played back into the focal text. It is in the brilliance of this playing that Derrida becomes genius-magician with his supporters noting only the genius and his enemies only the magician.

Such play, however, has implications for development. This may be seen in part by the very transformation of criticism as a new platform of deconstructionism. If what is first deconstructed is the text, the reflexive return is to deconstruct the activity of criticism itself. This double movement is succinctly described by Geoffrey Hartman in *Deconstruction and Criticism*. The first side of the movement is to disperse, as it were, the usual loci of meaning:

> Deconstruction, as it has come to be called, refuses to identify the force of literature with any concept of embodied meaning and shows how deeply such logocentric or incarnationist perspectives have influenced the way we think about art. We assume that, by the miracle of art, the "presence of the word" is equivalent to the presence of meaning. But the opposite can also be urged, that the word carries with it a certain absence or indeterminacy of meaning. Literary language foregrounds language itself as something not reducible to meaning; it opens as well as closes the disparity between symbol and idea, between written sign and assigned meaning.[4]

Here there is a deliberate gestalt switch which diffuses the usual sense of meaning towards its indeterminate horizon. Once meaning is dispersed in this way one can also reconceive the task of criticism itself. Criticism ceases to perform certain taken-for-granted functions and assumes a literature-like role itself, the critic elevates himself/herself to artist.

> These problems center on [the] issues that affect literary criticism today. One is the situation of criticism itself, what kind of maturer function it may claim—a function beyond the obviously academic or pedagogical . . . to insist on the importance of literature should not entail assigning to literary criticism only a service function.[5]

What occurs with literature and the critics may be taken as a paradigm of the general moves of the deconstructionists. The text, language, emerges as clearly *not* the invention of or expression of a subject. Nor does language remain tied to the World (although the more conservative thinkers influenced by the semiological strategy continue to speak of a "world" of the text, i.e., Ricœur) as its referendum. Instead, the text is a nexus of diffused and indeterminate meaning which can be explored virtually infinitely and particularly through the devices of decentered gestalt switches and refocuses upon what were previously taken to be fringe phenomena.

The implications of such tactics are immense, if indeterminate. No one can retain "control" of a text, neither author, reader or critic. Yet the desire for control remains a background feature as, for example, in Derrida's footnote which runs parallel with his text, "Living On: Border Lines," in *Deconstruction and Criticism*. To "control" a text would be to be able to explore all of its possibilities—but it is precisely this which deconstructionism has opened and thus in a sense placed beyond our grasp.

Meaning/language now runs wild, it exceeds or intentions and not unlike what some take to be autonomous technology, has become a "conceptual" or "literary" machine taking its own direction. Words have become an "abysm."[6] To return to the military campaign metaphor, this makes for an extremely elusive target. It is for that reason that a higher vantage point is needed.

III. Semiotics and the Philosophy of Language

In an excellent survey of recent theories of meaning, Charles Taylor distinguishes two primary tendencies in contemporary philosophy of language.[7] The one tendency, which he terms designative, is followed primarily by the analytic traditions. Its roots lie deep in empiricism and, following a reductionist strategy, it seeks to demystify language and reduce it to designative and derivative functions. The second tendency, associated with certain Continental traditions and rooted in the concern of Romanticism with language, he terms expressive. Here language retains a non-reducible sense of mystery and takes as its primitives, metaphors. Expressive theories are said to express some state of a subject and embody that state in an expression. Much of the warfare between contemporary analytic and phenomenological philosophers of language reflect this by now several century old division.

I should like to pick up on Taylor's distinctions and develop them in two directions. The first direction is one which locates two emphases already noted in phenomenology in contrast to deconstructionism. Designative or analytic philosophies often concentrated their theories upon the problem of *reference*. Thus I shall re-title Taylor's tendency towards designative functions, a reference theory. In this context, however, I am interested only in indicating that reference theory reverberates with the classical phenomenological concern with that to which reference refers: Thing and World. Granted, the concept of a thing and the world differs radically between empiricist (and Cartesian) grounded interpretations and phenomenology but it shares precisely that realist sense which was indicated above.

This may be seen symptomatically in the chosen paradigm discipline of inquiry favored by the analytic philosophies, i.e., the natural sciences. Philosophy was conceived of as "like" a science in some sense, minimally at least as a discipline which would preserve the possibility of a rigorous natural science. Again, although interpreted differently, this concern was also expressed in Husserlian phenomenology. I shall symbolize this concern as the aim of investigating natural phenomena, say the rings of Saturn. The problem of reference, then, is related to a concern with Things as the referenda. And from among these Things, chief are natural phenomena such as those investigated by science.

While phenomenology, particularly in its Husserlian form, may be seen to reciprocate with the analytic philosophies of language with respect to reference, its deeper concern lies with the other tendency in Taylor's distinction, expression. Phenomenology locates this tendency within its primary concern with *intentionality*. To explicate an expressive theory of language necessarily calls for some interpretation of intentionality. Thus subjectivity is implied and with it some sense of subject. Note that the problem of reference is not forgotten. It is now a subset of expressive theory insofar as intentionality is always directed (refers) towards *something*. But the "how" of this reference entails an interpretation of intention and intentionality. This concern permeates much phenomenological theory, whether in the form of Husserl's meaning acts or in the form of Heidegger's existentalia. Central to phenomenology is then a latent and sometimes explicit theory of language.

This theory of language, rooted in intentionality and focused upon expression, also reverberates with a paired discipline, in this case psychology. Expression is an action of a subject whether interpreted as "ego," "lived body," or "Dasein." There is thus a deep subterranean liaison between the analytic and phenomenological approaches to language, a liaison which on its "outward edge entails a realism of World and on its reflexive edge a realism of Self. Such approaches, in effect, reverberate with the paired disciplines of physics (and the natural sciences) and psychology (and some social or human sciences). The object of investigation remains in the first, World, in the return, Self.

Put in this way the appearance of semiotics must pose an enigma. But it is an enigma which has not been seen as clearly as it might have been precisely because semiotic developments were quickly absorbed in different ways by both analytic and phenomenological traditions. Here, however, I wish to accent and sharpen the contrast in tactics and results between semiotics on the one hand, and both analysis and phenomenology on the other. First, merely note that what was absorbed by the two contemporary movements differed according to their own internal tendencies.

Analytic philosophers, particularly those of formalist tendencies, were quick to adapt from semiology just those aspects which would absorb nicely into logical concerns. Thus the formalizable structural dimension was taken to be amenable to the notion that language is underlaid with (logical) structure. Phenomenological thinkers frequently seized upon the speech/language distinction and saw their work as elaborating the role and importance of speech acts, thereby saving aspects of their expressive theory of language.

This related, but differently accepted partial absorption of semiotics, however, blurs a deeper contrast between semiotics and both analysis and phenomenology. This contrast can be seen more clearly by taking note of a two-stage development within, first, structuralist semiotics, then its subsequent development in poststructuralist deconstruction.

The claims and aims of semiotics begin modestly. The distinctions originally developed by Saussure and refined by Hjelmslev, Jacobson and others were set in movements directed toward understanding language, strictly a linguistics. At first the tactics were directed toward what could be called the *constitution of a realm of objectivity*. Binary pairs of terms were developed, but with assymetrical weights. Thus the famous speech/*language*, diachrony/*synchrony*, etc., distinctions became part of a *system* for understanding language. The assymetrical concern (with the italicized member of the pair) with the move which constituted Language[8] in its semiotic sense as an object to be studied. Linguists clearly understood that both terms of the pair were "real" and operational in a life situation, but as with any science what is to be understood must be made to come to stand before one.

Language was being constituted as a kind of cultural *object*. Once successful as a method, however, the temptation to reification and elevation of the preferred emphases becomes almost irresistible. Thus one finds already in a structuralism a certain elevation of claim: language founds speech, synchrony grounds diachrony. Here we begin to drift towards an *ontology*. It was this tendency which Paul Ricœur detected early and which he opposed in the well-publicized debates with Levi-Strauss. Ricœur reasserted the other side of the pairs, speech and diachrony,[9] without denying the role of structure in experience and history. A higher level phenomenological interpretation of the tendency to move from the constitution of a realm of objectivity towards its subsequent reification might be called *the establishing of a perspective*. If, phenomenologically, all perspectives are valid, they also necessarily remain partial. For whenever the profile or "surface" of an object is seen there is also implied and latent in the perception the "backside" of the face towards one. To forget the latter is to reduce the thing.

If the first move of structuralist semiotics may be understood as constituting a realm of objectivity, a second move follows, perhaps with more subtlety and less obviousness. The full set of paired terms whenever fleshed out, constitute a *system* of understanding. And at least in some cases the semiological system tends toward a system of *internal relations*.

For purposes of this essay, I wish only to establish the tendency towards such a system. It is first a tendency to distance semiotics from both World and Self through and by means of the constituted system of terms. The tendency can be shown by noting that this distancing is implied by both sides of a certain aporia within semiology itself. What kind of "language" is semiotics? (The move here should be philosophically obvious—it is the usual self-referential move.) The answer frequently produces the aporia which on one side produces an infinite regress and on the other a closed system which in effect operates like a tautology. Both interpretations may be noted in Barthes's *Elements of Semiology*.

Barthes himself seems to favor the endless regress. The "language" of semiology is a metalanguage: "It is evident that semiology, for instance, is a metalanguage, since as a second-order system it takes over a first language (or language-object) which is the system under scrutiny; and this system-object is *signified* through the metalanguage of semiology."[10] Then begins the regress: "Nothing in principle prevents a metalanguage from becoming in its turn the language-object of a new metalanguage; this would, for example, be the case with semiology if it were to be 'spoken' by another science."[11] Presumably this ascent can go on *ad infinitum*.

My purpose here, however, is not to expose the philosophical problems internal to this move, but to establish the tendency to distance semiology from Things. By returning to the problem of reference this may be shown. Let us suppose that whatever first-order language is, it *refers*, points to or lets be seen some Thing (in this case not itself linguistic in nature). The very first step of a "linguistics" is one which no longer inquires after this Thing—its object of reference is itself now the linguistic first-order act of referring. Here not one, but two things have changed. First, the referent has changed and the act of referring substitutes for the Thing, and second the referring, while not disappearing, has "ascended" in this interpretation and operates at a metalinguistic level.

The tendency to distance from the Thing is now easily shown. If first-order language refers to the (nonlinguistic) Thing, then second-order language (semiotics) at most refers to the referring and any subsequent language (discussion of semiotics) refers to the referring of the referring. *Note that the very concept of a* metalanguage contains but submerges the notion of reference. Within semiotics reference is absorbed into the system of signifier-signified.

The other possibility for the aporia is to make semiotics a totally self-referential, closed system. In this case anything "external" in order to be admitted would have first to be "translated" into the approved language. And this is precisely what happens to the now vestigial Thing with respect to a semiological analysis.

Such a move is again amply illustrated by Barthes. In *Elements of Semiology,* the vestigal Things are fashions, the road system, food distribution, furniture. (Choices are rarely neutral. Why not choose the system of planets, the distribution of molecules in gases or some other noncultually accreted Things?) Fashion is taken as a (semiotic) system which "speaks" as a language. ". . . The fashion magazine . . . 'speaks' the significations of garments just as one speak a language . . ."[12] Here language has become metaphor (Barthes is aware of this) by which "Things" reenter the semiotic language world. But this is equivalent to saying that prior to dealing with Things they must first undergo translation. Once translated "Things" may now fit into the scheme and be interpreted in terms of an already established system. In this respect they operate as an element in a system of internal relations. I probably need not point out that any system of internal relations is in some sense "idealist" (at least in a Bradleyan sense). It is this tendency which another French philosopher, Levinas, opposes with his emphasis upon the totally other.[13]

Thus whether semiotics follows the tactic of the infinite regress, or goes the way of a totalized and self-referential system, its tendency is to move away from any first-order reference outwardly towards World or reflexively from self. In passing it should also be noted that the values which are preferred within the structuralist form of semiotics are also those of classical metaphysics in the West. Structure precedes or grounds history (synchrony

INTERPRETATION

over diachrony); shape or architechtonic over temporality, event or occasion (language over speech) and system over elements (from over content).

These values make up part of the implicit metaphysics of structuralism. And it is in just this dimension of structuralism that Derrida sees a debt to phenomenology (as he interprets it):

> That modern structuralism has grown and developed within a more or less direct and avowed dependence upon phenomenology suffices to make it a tributary of the most purely traditional stream of Western philosophy, which, above and beyond its anti-Platonism, leads Husserl back to Plato.[14]

Contrarily, phenomenology at least in Husserl's emphasis upon essence, is *structuralist*. If structuralist semiotics departs from the realism of Self and World, it remains linked to phenomenology insofar as it retains the internal sense of structure.

I wish to take one more step from this high altitude prior to returning to the immediacy of the battle between phenomenology and deconstruction. Sometime by taking note of the location and shape of a theory one can detect its trajectory more clearly. In this case one can do this by asking after the related and protected disciplines associated with the theories discussed. The question might be put in rather bald terms: *could there be a semiotic natural science?* My suspicion is that such a discipline would indeed be hard to develop. One might say that to date semiology has seen its methods as more clearly associated with what I shall call the cultural sciences—indeed it has frequently made claims that semiology is to the cultural sciences what physics has been for the natural sciences.[15] And on the surface, given its focus upon language and linguistics with languages understood at least as cultural objects, such a claim sounds more plausible than any claim to redevelop natural science. At least semiotics currently remains more proximate to a human science and more distant to a natural science. Is, then, the bald question inappropriate in that current semiotic self-awareness recognizes its limitations?

I am suggesting that theories have focuses, selectivities, and thus limitations. To stretch them too far is to make them at the least highly metaphorical, at most ludicrous. So, if semiology by virtue of its linguistic focus remains neighbor to the cultural sciences, one can rephrase the bald form of the question: how would semiotics deal with a natural science? The answer is: it would treat it as a semiotic system, a "language" with its set of oppositions, levels, etc. That is, semiotics can translate science as a first-order language into a (semiotic) cultural object. That is to say, semiotics can do a type of history and sociology of natural science in its own distinctive way—but it probably cannot *do* natural science. To do science, one would have to return to first-order reference which, for purposes here, necessarily entails *perception*. And perception entails intentionality because perception is always of _____.[16]

We now have located a certain trajectory and selectivity for semiotics. A cultural science which deals with institutionally constituted things (thus anthropology, politics, economics) is its appropriate field, and indeed, the most successful applications of semiotics outside linguistics have been in such areas. Such a location of a theory's shape suggests limits, but does not circumscribe them. It might be the case that there could be a semiotic physics, just as it might be the case that there could be a phenomenological neurology—but I suspect we are both far from these and that we would be able to develop such disciplines only by stretching insights metaphorically to a breaking point. Hume would have a hayday.[17]

Of course to a semiotic linguist, such reminders of what might be relevant might seem unnecessary. But there remains the temptation on the part of those who wish to elevate semiotics to philosophical status to ontologize the implicit metaphysics of structuralism. At the same time semiology also provides a background for a different development in what is today called post-structuralism, particularly in its deconstructionist phase. While post-structuralism shares with semiotics the silence about Self and World, it also reacts against precisely the structure of structuralism. Thus there appears to be an initial negative cast to post-structuralism. It seems more clearly outlined by what it is against

173

than its possible positive program. But here I shall redescend into the more immediate battle between phenomenology and deconstuctionism once again.

IV. Deconstruction and Phenomenology Redux

The moves I shall make in this section will be to show how deconstructionism—at least in its possibly best recognized figure, J. Derrida (Hartman's "boa-deconstructor"[18]) is in a fundamental sense dependent upon a phenomenological tradition. And yet its internal strategic demands simultaneously drive it to the kind of excess which marks the current situation.

In a crucial programmatic article, "Force and Significance," (1963) which opens *Writing and Difference* Derrida opens an attack upon both pheomenology and structuralism. It is a kind of rebellion against his intellectual parentage, and as a rebellion it is marked precisely by that against which the revolt is directed. The explicit enemy is classical or Western metaphysics. Derrida holds that metaphysics permeates both phenomenology and structuralism including even Heidegger's thought to which Derrida seems closest.

In such an attack, however, Derrida *repeats a tradition.* Phenomenology begins, one might say, in an attack upon metaphysics. Much of the elaborate machinery developed by Husserl is directed at a narrow version of metaphysics, Cartesianism. The moves of the reductions, epoché, and the change from a "natural" to a "phenomenological" attitude are all directed at getting us to see that the world is not as it is portrayed to be by Modern metaphysics. What is experienced is not an abstract, geometrized set of observed objects. These are given only to an observer consciousness which, ironically, is named the "natural attitude." For such objects, Husserl substitutes Things, that is, fully complex and multidimensioned objects of lived perceptions. The Husserlian attack upon metaphysics is upon reductionist strategies and the proliferation of hypothetical abstractions.

Heidegger continues this tradition, but his version of the enemy is more historical and broadly based. Modern metaphysics in its Husserlian context is but the latest arrival upon a scene which has its past in the very inception of classical Greek philosophy. Heidegger sees the fall into objects as a tendency of Platonic and Aristotelian logics, logics which reduce reason to a propositional form.

The famous call for a return to the question of Being was placed in the context of recovering what the Greeks "forgot." But in the process Heidegger also increasingly deconstructs Husserl's version of phenomenology. And although *Being and Time* was dedicated to Husserl, it can also be read as a severe attack precisely upon the vestiges of metaphysics which remain in Husserl's thought. The Husserlian transformation of (reduced) object into (phenomenological) Thing, Heidegger saw, retained not only the structure of the Cartesian focus upon objects, but left standing as the core of the Thing what could be called the *observed object*. More primitive and basic, Heidegger argued, was Dasein's praxis and everyday use of things which in turn grounded the possibility for a special case of use, observation. This existentialization of the Thing is symptomatic of the entire early Heideggerian strategy and marks his radicalization of phenomenology over Husserl.

In the process of Heidegger's deconstruction, however, Heidegger pointed up the limitations of the Greek *view* of things (in the above context he notes that the Greek notion of *pragmata* covers over the sense of use and confuses pragmata with observed objects. Thus the turn to the epistemological object is already latent with the Greeks.[19]) Heidegger sees Husserl as still captured by this tendency and thus it may be said that Heidegger deconstructs the vestigial Husserlian metaphysics.

Such is now the trajectory—a nascent tradition—of phenomenology. And it is this trajectory which Derrida takes up in his own way. One may almost say that Derrida is to Heidegger (and through him to Husserl) what Heidegger was to Husserl. Derrida both owes a central insight to and attempts to deconstruct a basic Heideggerian thesis. Derrida attacks the vestigial metaphysics in Heidegger which Derrida dubs the metaphysics of presence.

One can see both the debt to Heidegger and the unique way Derrida deals with it in Derrida's own characterization of metaphysics as photological:

> ... The founding metaphor of Western philosophy as metaphysics [is the metaphor of darkness and light.] The founding metaphor not only because it is a photological one—and in this respect the entire history of our philosophy is a photology, the name given to a history of, or treatise on, light—but because it is a metaphor. Metaphor in general, the passage from one existent to another, or from one signified meaning to another, authorized by the initial *submission* of Being to the existent, the *analogical* displacement of Being, is the essential weight which anchors discourse in metaphysics, irremediably repressing discourse into its metaphysical state.[20]

Derrida rightly sees that at least one side of Heidegger remains subject to the metaphor which guides Western metaphysics. The question of Being remains a play of presence and absence, light and darkness on the one side of Heidegger. There is, however, another side to Heidegger and this side is more positively taken up by Derrida and that is what may be called the Nietzschean side. It is here that we may begin to see what Derrida begins to reconstruct (and in this one may begin to sharpen one's own deconstructive weapons precisely because the now established antimetaphysics tradition remains a trajectory which can apply to Derrida as well).

The Nietzschean tone of "Force and Signification" is unmistakable. The *other* of presence is *force*. Note: "Force is the other of language without which language would not be what it is."[21] But Derrida is also wary and does not want to slip into the metaphysical trap, thus he must call for a yet more radical strategy to avoid his own vestige of metaphysics. This is why phenomenology as explicit strategy must be rejected:

> Force cannot be conceived on the basis of an oppositional couple, that is, on the basis of the complicity between phenomenology and occultism. Nor can it be conceived, from within phenomenology, as the *fact* opposed to *meaning*.

> Emancipation from this language must be attempted. But not as an *attempt* at emancipation from it, for this is impossible unless we forget *our* history. Rather as the dream of emancipation . . . as resistance to it as far as possible.[22]

How, then, is Derrida to be able to do his "saying of Being" to use a Heideggerian phrase? The answer is: he will write it. The tactic here is a gestalt switch, an inversion of primacies. If phenomenology is bound by its preferences to the precedence of speech and discourse (and hence to a Self), Derrida will assert the primacy of writing.

Such an inversion, on the surface, appears odd at the least, perverse at most. It strikes one as *counter-intuitive*. Historically (chronologically) speech clearly must come before writing; the "reduction" of spoken language to writing is relatively recent. How, then, can writing be primary?

The tactics Derrida uses to make his claim plausible are themselves deeply rooted in the phenomenological tradition. It is clear, although not always understood, that for Husserlian phenomenology *intuitions are constituted*. The inversion of both the sedimentations of common sense and science (the "natural attitude") and their replacement with the phenomenological field of possibilities ("Essences") could well be called a deconstruction of intuitions. This is not to say phenomenology is counter-intuitive, but it does situate or contextualize intuitions so that they can not be considered as "givens."[23] Early Derrida, in *Speech and Phenomena*, began his own attack upon what he considered to be Husserl's naïveté concerning speech. And while the attack there does not yet elucidate writing as privileged, he does apply the master's own deconstruction of the intuitive to Husserl himself.

Much more foundational for Derrida's deconstructive strategy, however, is Heidegger's version of a deconstructive ontology. As far as it may seem from the subject matter of current deconstructionism, it is Heidegger's "Question Concerning Technology" which shows the tactic later adapted by Derrida. In that essay, Heidegger grants the contemporary belief that (modern) technology is historically (chronologically) dependent upon Modern science. However, technology is claimed to be *ontologically* prior and only now is coming into view as the instrument by which Technology is seen for what it is, a total world view or "metaphysics."[24] In short, the paradoxical assertion is that science is historically prior, but technology is ontologically prior. Here we have what amounts to an isomorphism with Derrida's argument about writing.

While writing may be historically later, its ontological import precedes speech. Such is the import of the Derridean claim. But deconstruction implies reconstruction even if Derrida might deny it. There is no pure negative theology any more than there is a pure deconstruction. What the inversion does is to force us to look at writing in a different way. And that is exactly what Derrida does. In the earlier essays writing is linked with *inscription*.

Writing as force is *inscription*. For the recalcitrant photologist, picture a new Moses inscribing a tablet and this is not too far from the correct image as the Mosaic-Nietzschean closure to the essay:

> 'Behold, here is a new tablet; but where are my brethren who will carry it with me to the valley and into hearts of flesh?' [Or Derrida's own claim] Writing is the moment of this original Valley of the other within Being . . . Incidence and insistence of inscription.[25]

Inscription is an act of force. But, ironically, it might also be a *metaphysical* act of force.

Metaphysics is founded by a *metaphor*. And insofar as a metaphor both reveals and conceals, it displaces and represses Being into its metaphysical state.[26] The dominant Western metaphor, Heidegger and Derrida proclaim, is photological. But does a new tablet not do the same thing? Does it not attempt to inscribe a new metaphor? Is this not merely a new act of founding? If so, it is essentially metaphysical. Derrida says: "Writing is the outlet as the descent of meaning outside itself within itself: metaphor-for-others-aimed-at-others-here-and-now, metaphor as metaphysics in which Being must hide itself if the other is to appear."[27]

Here the aporia which lies at the heart of deconstructionism begins to appear. Derrida seems both to want to escape yet another reduction or repression of discourse, but at the same time to assert the privilege of what is clearly a new metaphor: writing. At first his strategy is to escalate claims for writing:

(1) In a deconstructive but weak claim, Derrida denies that meaning can exist alone. Through writing one discovers that, "It is also to be incapable of making meaning absolutely precede writing; it is thus to lower meaning while simultaneously elevating inscription."[28] Such an observation functions, in phenomenological terms, to locate meaning within its concrete background or field. Just as there are no perceived "x's" except in a field so (2) does meaning only occur in a context. "Meaning must await being said or written in order to inhabit itself, and in order to become, by differing from itself, what it is: meaning."[29] (3) However, Derrida also wants to claim a kind of privilege to writing. "It is because writing is *inaugural*, in a fresh sense of the word, that it is dangerous and anguishing . . . Writing is an initial and graceless recourse for the writer, even if he is not an atheist but, rather, a writer."[30] (4) But the kind of privilege Derrida wants, in an attempt to avoid a blatant metaphysics, lies in a kind of dialectic, a peculiar *secondarity*:

> . . . Is not the experience of *secondarity* tied to a strange redoubling by means of which constituted—written—meaning presents itself as prerequisitely and simultaneously *read*: and does not meaning present itself as such at the point at which the other is found, the other who maintains both the vigil and the back-and-forth motion, the work, that comes between writing and reading, making this work irreducible? Meaning is neither before nor after the act. Is not that which is called God, that which imprints every human course and recourse with its secondarity, the passageway of deferred reciprocity between reading and writing?[31]

Here is a peculiar metaphor, but one about which the privilege is clear. ". . . Paradoxically, inscription alone . . . has the power of poetry, in other words has the power to arouse speech from its slumber as sign."[32] In this sense it seems hard for Derrida to escape the charge that he presents us with a metaphysical function. But it is a function which he wants to be interpreted differently, to be interpreted as a kind of infinite tradition:

> [Inscription] creates meaning by enregistering it, by entrusting it to an engraving, a groove, a relief to a surface whose essential characteristic is to be infinitely transmissible. . . . Whether this project of an infinite tradition is realized or not, it must be acknowledged and respected in its sense as a project.[33]

The project's aim has been carried out. What has emerged is something like a Talmudic "metaphysics," a tradition in which there is no end to interpretation and criticism, a tradition in which the continued interpretation itself takes on privilege as the body of endless interpretation:

> If the play of meaning can overflow signification (signalization), which is always enveloped within the regional limits of nature, life and the soul, this overflow is the movement of the attempt-to-write. . . . In the extent to which the literary act proceeds from this attempt-to-write, it is indeed the acknowledgment of pure language, the responsibility confronting the vocation of "pure" speech which, once understood, constitutes the writer as such.[34]

How can writing be privileged and yet not repress the discourse as a new founding metaphor? Derrida's answer seems to be, by being endless discourse in interpretation and criticism. By becoming infinite tradition.

There is a problem and a price to be paid for such a position. The problem is: how can the privilege of writing be maintained without effectively making a metaphysical claim? The slippery escalation which first allows speech its place as an incarnation of meaning (along with writing before writing emerges as new metaphor) is one which can only be maintained by an ontological defense. Ontology underground remains ontology.

The price is: if writing unleashes the infinite surplus of possible meaning in an infinite tradition, not only is there no last word, there is only incessant word. And incessant word like the escalation of any chant, soon is endangered by its own monotony.

In this state deconstruction must stand precariously upon a not fully explicit metaphysics of the privilege of writing and simultaneously risk the self-invited deluge of discourse which is endless.

V. Conclusion: Phenomenological Deconstruction

I have tried to show how at least one contemporary example of deconstructionist thinking, the work of Derrida, owes a certain heritage to phenomenological deconstruction. His inheritance, of course, is multiple, but by combining the phenomenological "negative theology" of antimetaphysics with the semiological rejection of Self and World, the more radical "negative theology" of deconstructionism emerges.

Following this line of interpretation, however, I wish to close with a suggestion. Were one to follow the antimetaphysical tradition begun in Husserl, broadened by Heidegger and radicalized by Derrida, and direct that trajectory towards Derrida, I think there remains at least one basic and possibly foundational counterattack which might be made.

The aporia of writing as new founding metaphor seems the direct and most frontal place for assault. But I suggest there is a more effective tactic, a flank attack, which might more dismay the new army. That tactic would be an attack upon the very notion of metaphor which currently circumscribes the battle array. After all, the very notion of metaphor arose within metaphysics. It is dependent in its traditions upon the bifurcation between referential and expressive theories of language. And I suggest that to accept the notion of metaphor in its current guise is already to accept a metaphysical heritage.

Behind metaphor lies a desire for totality: to say all once and for all. The limit of metaphor, whether interpreted as analogy or as partial description, lies in its suggestive selectivity. It can repress only if it doesn't say everything, if it conceals as much as it reveals. It is the linguistic counterpart to a Husserlian stance before a perceptual profile, an *Abschattungen*. But what the profile ultimately revealed was the positive finitude of the perceiver. I suggest that to ultimately overcome metaphysics, what needs to be overcome is the false desire which remains symptomatic in the notion of metaphor. Metaphor hides a linguistic metaphysics which is not yet deconstructed.

Notes

Chapter Two

1. Technology, capitalized indicates a use similar to what Heidegger calls the essence of *technology*.
2. Martin Heidegger, "The Question Concerning Technology" in *Basic Writings*, trans. David Krell (New York: Harper and Row, 1977), p. 296.
3. *Ibid.*, pp. 302–3.
4. *Ibid.*, p. 304.
5. *Ibid.*, p. 296.
6. *Ibid.*
7. *Ibid.*, p. 303.
8. *Ibid.*, p. 288: "The current conception of technology, according to which it is a means and a human activity, can therefore be called the instrumental and anthropological definition of technology."
9. *Ibid.*, p. 294.
10. *Ibid.*
11. *Ibid.*
12. Lynn White, Jr. *Medieval Technology and Social Change* (Oxford University Press, 1962), p. 84.
13. *Ibid.*, p. 98.
14. *Ibid.*, p. 124.
15. *Ibid.*, p. 125.
16. Lynn White, Jr., "Cultural Climates and Technological Advance in the Middle Ages," *Viator* 2 (1971), 171.
17. *Ibid.*, p. 173.
18. *Ibid.*, p. 198: "In a separate building outside Hagia Sophia, Justinian placed a clepsydra and sundials, but clocks were never permitted

within or on Eastern churches; to place them there would have contaminated eternity with time. As soon, however, as the mechanical clock was invented in the West, it quick spread not only to the towers of Latin churches but also to their interiors."

19. *Ibid.*, p. 199.
20. *Ibid.*, p. 180.
21. A popular discussion of these techniques may be found in *National Geographic* 146, no,. 6 (December 1974), 732–781.
22. I call these existential relations. See chapter one of my book *Technics and Praxis* (Dordrecht: Reidel Publishers, 1979).

Chapter Four

1. Martin Heidegger, *Being and Time*, trans. J. Macquarrie and E. Robinson (New York: Harper and Row, 1962), p. 32.
2. David Hume in *The English Philosophers from Bacon to Mill*, ed. E. A. Burtt (New York: Random House, 1939), pp. 704–5.
3. *Ibid.*, p. 705.
4. *Ibid.*, p. 717.
5. *Ibid.*, p. 721.
6. *Ibid.*, p. 725.
7. *Ibid.*, p. 728.

Chapter Five

1. Edmund Husserl, *Ideas*, trans. W. R. Boyce Gibson (New York: Macmillan, 1958), sec. 70.
2. *Ibid.*
3. Edward Weston, *Daybooks* (New York: Aperture).

Chapter Seven

1. Maurice Merleau-Ponty, *The Visible and the Invisible*, trans. Alfonso Lingis (Evanston, Ill.: Northwestern University Press, 1968), p. 212.
2. *Ibid.*

3. *Ibid.*
4. For a full development of the notion of multi-stability see my *Experimental Phenomenology* (New York: G. P. Putnam's, 1977).

Chapter Eight

1. Martin Heidegger, *Being and Time*, trans. John Macquarrie and Edward Robinson (New York: Harper and Row, 1962), pp. 62–63.
2. *Ibid.*, p. 62.
3. Martin Heidegger, *Time and Being*, trans. Joan Stambaugh (New York: Harper and Row, 1973), p. 78.
4. Maurice Merleau-Ponty, *Phenomenology of Perception*, trans. Colin Smith (London: Routledge & Kegan Paul, 1962), p. xiv.
5. Martin Heidegger, *Discourse on Thinking*, trans. John M. Anderson and E. Hans Freund (New York: Harper and Row, 1966), p. 63, hereafter English; *Glassenheit* (Tübingen: Neske, 1959), p. 36, hereafter German.
6. English, p. 63; German, p. 36.
7. English, p. 64; German, p. 36.
8. English, p. 64; German, p. 37.
9. English, p. 64; German, p. 37.
10. English, p. 65; German, p. 38.
11. English, p. 72; German, p. 48.
12. English, p. 67; German, p. 41.
13. English, p. 67; German, p. 41.
14. English, p. 66; German, pp. 39–40.
15. English, p. 64; German, p. 37.
16. English, p. 65; German, p. 39.

Chapter Nine

1. Although the outline I have followed to this point is fairly familiar, I would refer the reader to a more detailed account of origins in Richard Palmer, *Hermeneutics: Interpretation Theory in Schleiermacher, Ditbey, Heidegger and Gadamer* (Evanston, Ill.: Northwestern University Press, 1969).
2. I consider my book, *Listening and Voice: A Phenomenology of Sound*

(Ohio University Press, 1976), to be a continuation of the hermeneutic tradition in this direction.
3. Richard Palmer, *Hermeneutics*, p. 15.
4. *Ibid.*, p. 19.
5. *Ibid.*, p. 20.

Chapter Ten

1. According to students, including Heidegger, Husserl's teaching was directed at "phenomenological seeing," usually utilizing rich examples. Such a technique is lacking in his written work.
2. To demonstrate how one operates phenomenologically was the aim of my *Experimental Phenomenology* (New York: G. P. Putnam's, 1977). Here the machinery gradually takes a background role.
3. This point is made by Kuhn's *The Structure of Scientific Revolutions* (Chicago: University of Chicago Press, 1970) and applies well in this instance as well.
4. G. Hartman, *Deconstruction and Criticism* (New York: Continuum, 1979), pp. vii–viii.
5. *Ibid.*, p. vii.
6. *Ibid.*, p. ix.
7. Charles Taylor, "Theories of Meaning," *Man and World* 13, no. 3–4 (1980), 281–303.
8. I use Language, capitalized, to refer to the object language or body of language in contrast to language as *langue*.
9. See the second and third chapters of Riccoeur, *The Conflict of Interpretations* (Evanston, Ill.: Northwestern University Press, 1974).
10. Roland Barthes, *Elements of Semiology* (New York: Hill and Wang, 1967), p. 92.
11. *Ibid.*, p. 93.
12. *Ibid.*, p. 92.
13. Levinas attacks all immanentisms; see Derrida's critique in chapter four of *Writing and Difference* (Chicago: University of Chicago Press, 1978).
14. Jacques Derrida, *Writing and Difference* (Chicago: University of Chicago Press, 1978), p. 27.
15. That of which semiotics can properly deal might be called institutional. This includes language and cultural systems.
16. Referential theories implicitly presuppose that ultimate referen-

tiality, perception. Perception permeates both language and other "tool" systems such as technologies. See my *Technics and Praxis* (Dordrecht: Reidel Publishers, 1979).

17. I refer here to Hume's well-known attack upon arguments from analogy.

18. *Deconstruction and Criticism*, p. ix.

19. Martin Heidegger, *Being and Time* (New York: Harper and Row, 1962), pp. 96–97. See my chapter nine in *Technics and Praxis*.

20. *Writing and Difference*, p. 27.

21. *Ibid*.

22. *Ibid*., p. 28.

23. The "myth of the given" has frequently, but wrongly, been laid at Husserl's door. The "given" is, however, used by Husserl only as a kind of index for a starting point.

24. Martin Heidegger, "The Question Concerning Technology" in *Basic Writings*, trans. David Krell (New York: Harper and Row, 1977), pp. 295–304.

25. *Writing and Difference*, p. 30.

26. *Ibid*., p. 27.

27. *Ibid*., p. 29.

28. *Ibid*., p. 10.

29. *Ibid*., p. 11.

30. *Ibid*.

31. *Ibid*.

32. *Ibid*., p. 12.

33. *Ibid*.

34. *Ibid*., pp. 12–13.

Index

Abschatuungen, 128, 181
aesthetic stance, 61
aletheia, 32–33
Aristotle, 83, 138

Bacon, Roger, 34
Barthes, Roland, 170

Cage, John, 95
cogitatum, 124, 147
cogito, 11, 13, 147
Columbus, Christopher, 41
Copernicus, Nicolaus, 27
correlation-apriori, 123–24, 146–47
Critical Theory, 9
Crusades, 40
Cubism, 96

daFortuna, Giovanni, 34, 45
daVinci, Leonardo, 36
deconstruction, 4, 92, 95, 175
  deconstructionism, 163–64, 167
  deconstructionists, 159, 162, 165
Democritus, 26, 139
Derrida, Jacques, 4, 163–64, 166, 172, 174–81
deSaussure, Ferdinand, 168
Descartes, Rene, 11, 17, 65, 141–42
Dewey, John, 2, 9, 47

Edison, Thomas, 49
Enlightenment, 29

Epicurus, 138
essences, 83, 85, 94
existentialism, 9
existential praxis, 14, 16–22
existential thesis, 73

Foucault, Michel, 162
Freud, Sigmund, 150
functionalism, 45

Galileo, 27, 36, 39
geometric method, 12
Geschichte, 31
Greek science, 25–26

Hamann, Johann Georg, 153
Heidegger, Martin, 4, 10–11, 26, 29–32, 36–39, 50, 66, 76–77, 106, 119–26, 129–35, 144–45, 149–50, 153–54, 174–75, 177–78, 181
hermeneutics, 54, 61, 87, 120, 137–142, 149–157
hermeneuein, 137
Hermes, 137, 153
Higher Criticism, 139–40
Historie, 31
Hjelmslev, Louis, 168
horizon, 121, 123, 128–33, 135, 165
Hume, David, 66–71, 76, 173
Husserl, Edmund, 4, 12–13, 83–85,

Index

Husserl, Edmund (*Continued*)
  94, 119–20, 122–24, 141–49,
  161–62, 167, 172, 174–75, 181

imago, 72
Industrial Revolution, 27, 34
inscription, 178–80
intentional fallacy, 157
intentionality, 13, 53, 55, 124, 144–46, 167
intersubjectivity, 143
intuitional demonstration, 83
invariant, 14, 18, 70

Jacobson, Roman, 168
James, William, 2
Jonas, Hans, 10

Kennedy, John F., 61
Kepler, Johannes, 27, 39

Latin West, 35
Levinas, Immanuel, 171
Levi-Strauss, Claude, 169
Lucretius, 139

Marx, Karl, 9, 150
Marxism, 1, 9
Mead, George Herbert, 2
Merleau-Ponty, Maurice, 4, 109, 112
Modern Philosophy, 65, 71, 141
Monet, Claude, 81

Necker Cube, 90–92, 95, 112–13
Newton, Isaac, 27
Nietsche, Friedrich, 150
noema-noesis, 3, 126, 129–32, 146–48, 162

Oracle of Delphi, 137
Ordinary Language, 144
Oresmus, Nicholas, 34

Palmer, Richard, 155–56
Plato, 82, 172
poeisis, 32, 153–54
Polo, Marco, 40
Polynesian navigators, 42–44
Positivism, 2
Pragmatism, 9
praxis, 16, 25, 45, 73
  praxis philosophies, 9

Renaissance, 27–29, 45, 110, 139
Richardson, William, 119
Ricoeur, Paul, 144–45, 148–53, 157, 165, 169

Sartre, Jean-Paul, 9
Schleiermacher, Friedrich, 140
semiology, 156
Speigelberg, Herbert, 119

Taylor, Charles, 166–67
technē, 32
topography, 4, 90, 93, 114
Tortelli, Giovanni, 36

Vader, Darth, 162
variational method, 4, 14, 17–18, 70, 82–89, 94–95, 97
Versenyi, Lazlo, 119
Vikings, 42

Weston, Edward, 95
White, Lynn, Jr., 26–29, 33–36

www.ingramcontent.com/pod-product-compliance
Lightning Source LLC
Chambersburg PA
CBHW051100230426
43667CB00013B/2376